# I LOOK
# CRAZY
## BUT,
## IT'S GOD

*Jameson M. Eichelberger*

*I LOOK CRAZY, BUT IT'S GOD*

Copyright 2023 by Jameson M Eichelberger

**Credits:**
 Proofreading by BirthWork Publishing
 CopyEditing by Yuvelca Magdalena Reyes
 Graphic Designs by Estelle J Design

Oak Strong Publishing Company

The contents of this book are writings from the eye of the authors.

Printed in the United States of America.

# ACKNOWLEDGMENT

I dedicate this book to my Lord and Savior, Jesus Christ, whose influence from the Kingdom of God has made it possible for me to share this work with the world.

A heartfelt thank you goes to my incredible wife and life partner, Tomecka. Throughout this entire process, you have been my unwavering rock. When I felt like giving up, you showered me with strength, love, and encouragement and your praises always bring a smile to my face. I cannot express in words how much I love you.

To my beloved children, Jamiya, Jameson Jr., and Joseph, I am grateful beyond measure for the blessing of having you in my life. Your presence brings joy and purpose to my days. I want to express my deepest gratitude to my mother and father, Brenda and Major McDonald. Your love and encouragement have saved my life in more ways than one.

A special acknowledgement goes to Bishop Paul L. Fortson, whose guidance and support have impacted my life profoundly. You have been a true source of strength and inspiration. The lessons I have learned from you will forever be engraved in my heart. Thank you for being a man of God and for everything you have done for me. Your legacy will endure through the lives you have touched, and I am honored to be among them.

# FOREWORD

In a world ensnared by the shackles of conformity and suffocated by the weight of societal expectations, there exists an unconventional force that awakens a chord of bewilderment within the hearts of onlookers. It is within this perplexing tapestry of contradictions that we find ourselves confronted with a profound dilemma—the choice between leading a life deemed acceptable by others, carefully crafted to fit their image of who we should be, or embarking on a daring odyssey in pursuit of a destiny that aligns with our true purpose, a purpose divinely ordained by a higher power.

Through the insightful words of Prophet Eichelberger, we are challenged to reflect upon the moments when we dismissed the whispers of God as too extravagant, too "crazy" to be divine. We are urged to confront the fears that hold us back and to embrace the audacious call that resounds within our hearts.

In these pages, you will discover the power of walking by faith, where every step taken is divinely ordained, and every word spoken carries the weight of purpose. You will be reminded that God shows no partiality, and that if we surrender ourselves completely, even the most extraordinary dreams and visions can become our reality.

As you embark on this reading journey, I implore you to open your mind, heart, and spirit to the limitless possibilities that await you. May the words on these pages inspire you to step outside the confines of your comfort zone, to confront the doubts that hinder your progress, and to ignite the flame of hope that burns within.

Know that it is never too late to answer the call for the assignment God has placed upon your life. Embrace each step, each word, and trust that the path you walk, though it may appear crazy to others, is divinely ordained.

Prepare to be challenged, motivated, and empowered as you immerse yourself in the profound wisdom of Prophet Eichelberger. May this book serve as a catalyst for transformation propelling you towards a life of purpose fully fulfilled.

Remember, hope seen is not hope at all. Embrace the unconventional for within it lies the extraordinary. May your journey through these pages bring you closer to the realization of your God-given potential.

*Charlie A. Fortson*
BBA, MBA, MSIT, JD, LLM

# Contents

# INTRODUCTION

Life is a journey that we figure out as we live it out. Challenges, changes, and crises are woven into this fabric of living. There are no road maps to it but there is insight from others; within the wisdom and experiences life gives you. These past eight to ten years of my life have been absolutely crazy. Crazy in a good way. I want to empower you as your eyes fall upon these pages that God will break every doubtful thought of who He is in your mind.

I am a witness. Life will smack you in the mouth and won't even apologize. Mike Tyson said, "Everyone has a plan until they get punched in the mouth." Such is life. We have plans until life happens. Maybe you've been doubting yourself, discounting yourself, and downplaying the grace and the charisma of God that rests on you.

Grace is the ability, the fingerprint of God on you, to do what you were designed to do. You may have been searching for answers, like hidden treasure, and have come up empty-handed. New connections didn't pan out like you thought they would because you were looking for the answers to people when, truthfully, you are the answer.

What God has placed in your heart seems impossible, unbelievable, and crazy. When God made you he designed you to fit the piece of the puzzle that no one else has. You wasted countless hours looking for people to help you, but God was patiently waiting for you to believe him for the ridiculous and crazy. He was watching for your response to the call and assignment.

Are you a caged lion?

I will explain what I mean later.

God is commissioning us to step into the assignment and discover what we think is impossible that can only become possible with Him. There is no road map for believing God, for believing the impossible. You may look crazy but trust God with your life. This is a journey of faith, where the meaning of your life is displayed in your walk with God. On this journey, you will discover the person you will become. Pain and challenges usually point you to God's purpose. It's not always spelled out for you but there is an indicator inside of you that keeps going off as you get closer to Him. And the voice in you roars, it utters, it emits a full loud prolonged sound, it sings, it shouts with full force. Furthermore, it prognosticates with passion the assignment that was built in your DNA.

*The wicked flee though no one pursues, but the righteous are as bold as a lion (Proverbs 28:1 KJV)*

I learned something interesting about lions. Lions that are caged or born in captivity, if not returned to their natural habitat, will begin to use less of their natural abilities. They begin to lose the instinct to hunt. One thing in particular is the lion's roar. Lions roar to communicate their location to show their strength and to intimidate enemies from coming close to their dens.

Furthermore, a lion roars because it's covering its territory. When the lion is caged, it does not roar as much because there is no territory to cover, nor is there any enemy to run off. Caged lions will soon become docile. A docile posture isn't the behavior or attitude of a lion. A cage is a place where instincts are dulled and purpose fades. However, instinct is there, the DNA is there, just the environment has stifled who and what he is in the animal kingdom.

A person without a voice will soon become a purpose with no power. A voiceless person will remain stagnant and stuck. The lion's roar is just as important as his purpose or commanding presence. After hearing a lion roar, it would feel strange not to hear him roar again. Why? Because we know that's what they are known for. Imagine a voiceless lion! How strange and bizarre would that be! Now imagine a voiceless visionary, leader, athlete, or entrepreneur who never uses their voice or never steps out beyond their borders! How strange is that?

A voice is what John the Baptist was to Jesus, the forerunner of destiny. He spoke to the world declaring and prophesying what was and was to come. His purpose went before Jesus and told the world He was coming. Now what if John Baptist knew what he was designed for but never declared it or never lived it out? What if he would have let his environment steal his purpose and question what he was designed for? Let me make an announcement: You will show up in your place of purpose when you embrace your God's DNA. The voice, if you will, is your roar, the sounding board that propels you, identifies you, labels and strengthens you. It is the sound, the volume, and the vibration of the inner you that makes you unique. What you put your hands to and what comes from your lips characterizes you. It's amazing that there are a billion people and each of us has a distinct sound. We may sound similar but after careful observation you can clearly differentiate your voice from anyone else's voice. You may look crazy walking this out but you will know it's God.

This roar can not be ignored. Lions roar to warn lions from other prides to keep away from their home territory. That roar says, "This is where I am. This is where I will be and I am not moving!" You must fortify yourself when it comes to you, where you stand, and what you're called to do.  But I want to tell you that there's a new wave of glory coming to you. It's a fresh wind to confirm, comfort, and complete the assignment that is already in your life.

Dig deep my friend; I promise you it's there.

This leads me to prophetically declare: God says, "I am pouring out My Spirit upon you. I am activating what has been lying dormant, and I am giving you the supernatural ability to do what naysayers, demonic voices, and hindrances said you couldn't do. I know you thought it was impossible to think you could change the world with your voice. But all things are possible with God! I am giving you the gift to make a difference in your area of influence. Don't compare yourself to others because what I have planned is for you."

What the spectators and agitators are saying doesn't matter, but your expression on the earth does. You're about to surprise yourself. The prophetic temperature in your life is getting ready to be turned up to supernova. I declare that you will not be the same after the completion of the book. Every voice of restraint, every demonic muzzle, every satanic gag order to shut down your voice and assignment is broken, in the name of Jesus Christ. The world is waiting on you.

*Jameson M. Eichelberger*

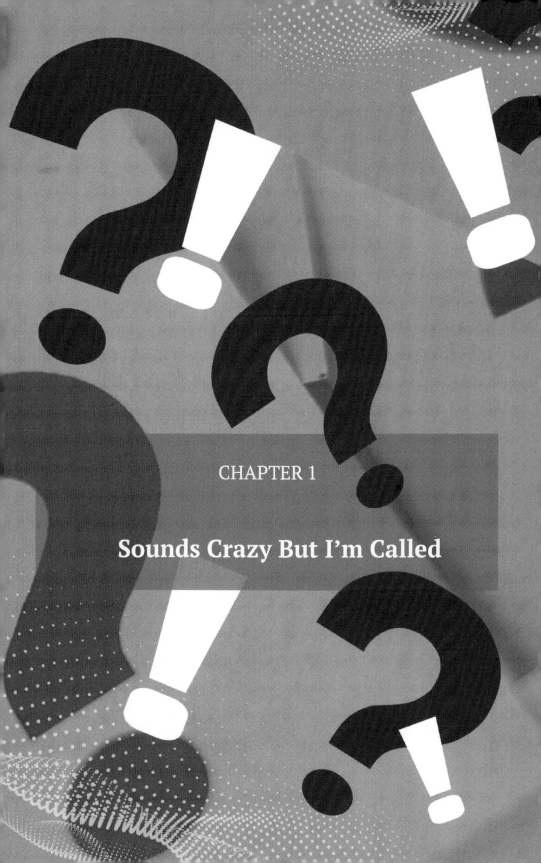

# CHAPTER 1

# Sounds Crazy But I'm Called

Life presents things that you can never imagine would happen. We, in our minds, have our whole life kind of planned out. Then God happens, change happens. He comes out of nowhere and lands you in a place called purpose. Please hear me!

I am just this guy that God picked out of nowhere to use. There's nothing I think that's great about me, but I've always felt something was in me to do great things. I couldn't tell you what it was if I tried. When I was a little boy I would lay in my mom's car while she was driving and in the back seat, looking at the stars in the sky, I wondered why I was here. I'm very clear that God doesn't need me. I need him! Why else would God take a young man from the projects, from being poor, in gangs and drugs, and see fit to use him? I often say, "I'm not the sharpest knife in the drawer but I'm not dumb either".

I have enough sense to know when God's hand is on something. How do you explain a person who has twenty four hours to live and this issue, concern, situation or circumstance that was going to kill them...disappears? Within twenty four hours? How can you explain that? Also how do you explain a person that came from nothing, no education, and no money yet has an undeniable charisma being used by God to change a generation? The supernatural can not be explained even though I have the education, the pedigree, and the grace. It's God.

One of the tough places where I looked crazy was when I accepted Jesus as Lord and Savior. It was a place of uncertainty, skepticism, and doubt. There is a backstory. The truth is I had an issue with God. My mother at the time was divorced, and raising two kids was difficult. We lived in a housing project for a while and I saw my mom struggle -walking to work, sweating from the heat, wrapping up in the cold, and never quitting. She was mistreated on the job yet never quit and continued to love God.

I remember seeing only water in the refrigerator and a block of cheese from welfare. During those times you would pick up food from the welfare office like cornflakes, powdered eggs, powdered milk, cheese, King Vitamin, and my favorite peanut butter with a white label and black letters on the can that said: PEANUT BUTTER. You would open it, there would be oil on the top of it, and you would stir it up to make it smooth. For those of you who don't quite know what I am talking about, it was a way the government took care of people with low-income to no income.

Sometimes we had to use water for our cereals because there was no milk. We had to make mayonnaise sandwiches, ketchup and syrup sandwiches because there was no meat. Seeing all of this through the eyes of a kid, I didn't know we were poor until 'life punched me in the mouth' at school. Nevertheless, my mother held on to her faith in God, provided for her children, and never deserted her faith or us. Just thinking back on it, that pain that aches creeps into my soul. I remember only having a few shirts and pants to wear for school at times and feeling rejected, lost, abandoned -what seemed like every day- and fighting at school because the kids gave me a hard time.

I was angry and did not understand why I wasn't like some of the other kids who had good clothes, friends, and the teachers who loved them. I felt like I was dirt on the bottom of their shoes. I would often stare at the sky wondering why I am here. Will it always be like this?

Those unfavorable moments were not the majority of my life. We had a great family that loved us, even in those times, we had more good days than bad. My mother was doing the best she could; she believed in God. However, to express the full impact of my life's transformation, I must share something very traumatic that almost made me give up on life and God.

Years later, my only sister at the time, Stephanie was murdered. She was shot execution-style in the head and left on the side of the road like a dead dog. I remember the last time I saw her. I was ironing my clothes and she dropped by the house to see us. Smiling like she always did, she peeked into the room and said, "Jameson, what are you doing tonight?"

I replied, "Hanging out with my friends".

She'd always say, "You got a girlfriend, yet?", laughing.

My reply was, "No, I am not sweating no girlfriend", then asked her what her plans were.

She said, "Going shopping!", then left the room to talk to my mother and stepfather.

Little did I know that it would be the last time I would see that smile and hear the constant jokes about not having a girlfriend.

The next morning I remember hearing the phone ring in my mom's room. That moment I won't share but it was the most eery painful moment to see. My mom had come into my room frantic with a face of dread and uncertainty saying, "They found Stephanie on the side of the road, dead".

My heart sank, my mind began to race, and fear gripped my heart as if I was falling into a deep dark hole. We drove to the location only to find out what was said over the phone was actually true. We cried in the car all the way home. I felt so helpless, hurt, defeated, angry, and confused, even to this day this hurts badly.

Writing this, I had to stop a few times to get myself together. Yet more news came. On top of finding Stephanie that same day, the husband committed suicide. So it was a murder-suicide. I remember going to the house afterward to gather my sister's belongings and seeing the hole in the wall from where the husband had killed himself - the blood, skull, and brain fragments were on the carpet. I was mortified, numb to any pain for him. It was as if I was walking through a graveyard and all I could sense was death!

During this grieving period, I walked the streets many nights alone, hurt. All kinds of thoughts flooded my mind as I walked and cried. How can a good God allow this to happen to my mom who I know loves Him? I didn't understand, and I had an issue with God for a long time.

Before and during this time, I really got more involved in selling drugs and more involved with the neighborhood gang 2.7.4. or BGD (black gangster disciples). I knew deep down it wasn't me. I was just a young kid from Mississippi ("The Sip") and my mom didn't raise me to be that way.

Years later, I moved to Atlanta to go to school and do music. I completed school but was deep in gangsta rap. Some time passed, I got married and started raising a family, left the drugs and gangs trap but was still into my music. My music career was taking off but my marriage was very much on the decline. I hadn't been to a church in what seemed like a decade.

My mother calls me one day and tells me, "Son, you need to start going to church, maybe that will help the marriage".

I did go but I didn't care too much for the church we visited. Now it's going to get a little crazy because something happened to me that I never told my wife about. There was a woman that my wife had become close with, who started a small daycare in her house. For two years, we took our children to her daycare services. On my way to pick them up, I would pass by a church that was set on a hill. While passing the church, I would turn my music down out of respect for the church. It was just what we did when I was growing up. We didn't play loud music when we came across a church and we didn't cuss. I had what we called 'a beat in my trunk'. I promise you I am not making this up.

When I would pass this church, I would hear a voice calling my name, "Jameson". My hair would stand up on my arms. I know it sounds crazy. I get you might think I am tweaking, but I wasn't. I hurried up to quickly turn my music's volume back up. Seriously, for two years, that was happening. I would be afraid to turn my music down. I wouldn't hear it every day, but I would hear my name being called.

Now let's go back and rewind because this is going to make sense, in a moment. Now remember, my mom was in Mississippi and I was in Atlanta. She had called me a few weeks after she heard that I didn't like the church I visited. This time my mom told me that there was a woman in Atlanta who wanted to invite us to their church. I was reluctant but I told my mom okay. I had no intentions whatsoever to do anything related to God but went anyway because my wife and my mom thought it would help my marriage. My wife contacted the woman. Keep in mind, we never met her before in our life.

Sunday comes. We print out directions. We start driving and guess where we pull up? The church! The church that has been calling my name for years. I was tripping: "What is going on?" "How can this be?"

I was nervous and anxious, at the same time sweating. I couldn't believe it. I was all mixed up like a Rubik's cube. Keep in mind, I hadn't said anything to my wife because she probably would have thought I was high. I can hear her now, saying, "Oh somebody calling your name, huh? Yeah, right!"

When we walked through the door something hit me. I can't explain it but a fear came over me. We went inside the church; we sat way in the back. I scanned the room, in the choir stand, I saw a cousin of mine I hadn't seen in years. On top of that, I didn't even know he was in Atlanta. All kinds of things went running through my head like maybe my wife and my own mom got together to set me up. I was tweaking, this had to be a dream. I know it sounds crazy, but I was about to have an encounter with God.

The Sunday morning service ended; we were making our way out the back door when all of a sudden this woman came running to the back and asked us if we were the Eichelberger's. We replied, "Yes", exchanged pleasantries, and then this woman said, "Let me take you to meet the bishop of the church". In my mind I was like, "Nahhh, this is not the move". Yet out of respect for this woman of God, we went to meet him. We shook hands with the bishop, he introduced himself, and turned to me and said, "Are you saved?" I knew what this meant: have you accepted Jesus as Lord and Savior?

I replied to him, "No!"

"Do you want to be saved", he asked.

"No!"

He turned to my wife and asked her the same thing, but her reply was, "Yes!" She wanted to give her life to Jesus.

Thoughts were running rampant in my mind, "How is this going to work, we're already on two different pages?". Unbeknownst to me, God was about to save my life and my marriage, at the same time.

The bishop told my wife, "You *been* praying for your husband."

She grabbed her face then burst into tears. While shaking her head, she said, "YES!" and started to cry.

I was shocked because first, how did he know this and secondly, I had never seen my wife pray a day in her life. In my head, I was like, "What!! Who told you to pray for me? You know what I am trying to do in this music". I was confused. I was not selling drugs. I was not doing any street stuff anymore and my wife was still not satisfied. The pastor prayed with my wife and led her to the Lord Jesus. Me? I just stood there looking like what in the world just happened.

After a moment, this man of God turns to me and says, "Son, if you don't wanna be saved, it's okay. Just let me pray for you". I replied with an okay you can pray for me. Then the strangest thing began to happen as he prayed for me. I became very angry, so angry to the point I was cursing in my mind. I was ready to fight; I was that angry. Yet, I began to get weak as if someone was taking all my strength away; it was his praying.

"Listen to me", said the pastor, "if you want to be saved, can you make the confession right now?" By this time, I was so weak that all I could do was whisper, yes. We prayed. Something came over me. It felt like thousands of little, tiny men dancing on my head. I didn't know at that time what it was. Now I know it was the Holy Spirit.

Before this realization, I had fallen to the floor in a fetal position, crying my eyes out. I must be honest. When I got up off the floor, I was embarrassed. My wife had never seen me cry and WHY in the heck was I crying? Sheesh!! I remember as I began to get up off the floor I heard this voice again say, "I am going to use you". At that very moment, the life I once lived was over. I know it sounds crazy, but it's God. Here I am months later living the best I know how.

Friends had asked me to come to the studio and get back to music. It was my love. However, I made a choice to not go back and separate myself from anyone or anything that was pulling me backwards. Those moments were critical. The thoughts of turning back to my former life flooded my head. Doubts came, even now, but what I thought of more is not quitting in following the purpose of God. The enemy knows that not serving Jesus isn't an option, especially when you have experienced Jesus. However it will not stop the enemy from getting you to turn down the wrong road as much as possible. It is a trick the enemy uses. Don't get distracted; fix your eyes on Jesus.

Jesus was even tried by the enemy to turn from his assignment. "If thou be the Son of God," he said, "cast thyself down: for it is written, He shall give his angels charge concerning thee: and in their hands they shall bear thee up, lest at any time thou dash thy foot against a stone." (Matthew 4:6 KJV)

Jesus answered him, "It is written again, Thou shalt not tempt the Lord thy God" (Matthew 4:7 KJV)

There are things that look good or seem innocent that can detour your destiny and it can take decades to get you rerouted. I remember a story of Kathryn Kuhlman. She married the wrong man and it set her ministry back for ten years. It serves as a reminder that doing what you want versus doing what God wants is unwise on all levels because he knows what's best.

There is a difference between anointing and ambition. Anointing is God's hand on you to do it effortlessly. Ambition is your hand on it with all your efforts. One will guide you with peace because it doesn't come from you, the other will have you up at night trying to figure out your next move. 'Lean not on your own understanding', right?

I will never forget the moment God spoke to me. I was working the night shift alone on a Sunday going through this period of separation where friends and family became very distant. I had seriously given my life to God and my usual friends didn't want to be around me anymore. They understood I was no longer doing what they were doing. My coming to the Lord was radical because God was doing quick work on me. That night I was very depressed and despondent, a lot of things were running through my mind. I began to wonder whether I had made the right choice. Was this living for Jesus? Being lonely, depressed, and being friendless? I got up, walked outside the building, and sat on a garbage dumpster. I looked up, stared at the stars, and began to talk to God. Well, really to complain, I felt isolated. I cried out, "God, what do you want from me? I'm just a child in God and new to this living for God thing!"

Just as soon as I said those words, I heard the Lord say to me, "Sit down and turn to Jeremiah first chapter and start at the 4th verse". It took every bit of three minutes to find that scripture.

I was walking back inside, to sit down, and open my bible. I was in awe of what I heard and turned to Jeremiah first chapter and started at the fourth verse. I felt a presence that was calming yet powerful. I often tell people that I heard the voice of God. I know it sounds crazy, right?

All the other times I heard this voice - like when I passed by the church and got up off the ground after crying from feeling the power of God - everything was totally different. This was clearer and full of warmth. It was stronger yet encouraging. I couldn't tell you if it was audible or inner, but it overtook me. I knew it was God and I wasn't afraid. I was fearful of reverence, knowing that he heard me.

What you need to keep in mind is that I didn't know any bible or scripture verses well enough to find anything. He said to turn to Jeremiah in the first chapter and start at the fourth verse. I promise I am not making this up.

> *"Then the word of the Lord came unto me, saying,*
> *Before I formed thee in the belly I knew thee; and*
> *before thou camest forth out of the womb I sanctified*
> *thee, and I ordained thee a prophet unto the nations.*
> *Then said I, Ah, Lord God! behold, I cannot speak:*
> *for I am a child." (Jeremiah 1:4-6 KJV)*

As soon as I read the sixth verse, I knew God was listening to every word I had said. Previously when I cried out to God in my helplessness, I knew God wanted me to do something but I just didn't know what. So I continued to read:

> *"But the Lord said unto me, Say not, I am a child: for thou shalt go to all that I shall send thee, and whatsoever I command thee thou shalt speak. Be not afraid of their faces: for I am with thee to deliver thee, saith the Lord. Then the Lord put forth his hand, and touched my mouth. And the Lord said unto me, Behold, I have put my words in thy mouth. See, I have this day set thee over the nations and over the kingdoms, to root out, and to pull down, and to destroy, and to throw down, to build, and to plant. Moreover the word of the Lord came unto me, saying, Jeremiah, what seest thou? And I said, I see a rod of an almond tree. Then said the Lord unto me, Thou hast well seen: for I will hasten my word to perform it." (Jeremiah 1:7-12 KJV)*

I was so awed by what I read. I remember that I stopped, jumped up out of my seat, put my back up against a wall, and started to look around the office. I knew God was there. I was nervous because I knew nothing about speaking to anyone, let alone being called a prophet, and had no clue what a prophet was.

After a few minutes, I calmed myself down and said, "God how are you going to do this?" I then added, "God, do you know who I am? Do you know the things I have done? How are you going to do this? How are you going to do this with me?"

This was my burning bush experience like that of Moses.

Once again God said, "Sit down and turn to Jeremiah the eighteenth chapter and read."

Now, as I mentioned earlier, I didn't know what the content was in Jeremiah. As I began to read, I was blown away that God could answer me that quickly.

> *"The word which came to Jeremiah from the Lord, saying, Arise, and go down to the potter's house, and there I will cause thee to hear my words. Then I went down to the potter's house, and, behold, he wrought a work on the wheels. And the vessel that he made of clay was marred in the hand of the potter: so he made it again another vessel, as seemed good to the potter to make it. Then the word of the Lord came to me, saying, O house of Israel, cannot I do with you as this potter? saith the Lord. Behold, as the clay is in the potter's hand, so are ye in mine hand, O house of Israel." (Jeremiah 18:1-5 KJV).*

Shock and amazement gripped me; I had to pull myself together. I was nervous, my eyes said I was afraid yet they stayed still, and glued to the pages for about five minutes. This encounter with God forever changed my life. I remember keeping those types of experiences to myself for fear that no one would ever believe me. I felt like this had to be hidden. No one was going to believe that I hadn't been with God but for a short while, yet not long enough to know anything. After a month or two I finally told my wife.

It took me every bit of six months to confide in a friend named Mark Brown, whom God had sent to help me. He was my Jonathan; I was his David in this situation. He showed me how to lean into my calling and not be afraid of it. Just like David from the scriptures who was a shepherd boy chosen to be king. He knew nothing about being king and what it took to be a great king. God connected him with Jonathan, the son of a king, in order to teach David about kingship. They had a covenant relationship like Minister Mark Brown had with me.

It would take me two years before I summoned up enough courage to share my encounter with my pastor. It was during a bible study where I was so nervous because I knew "my mess", but I also had heard God. When I shared my encounter with my pastor it was as if God had already spoken to him about it. He was welcoming and it encouraged me. He threw his arms onto my shoulder and said, "I am glad you obey God, son. I have been waiting on you."

Wow, that was a relief. I didn't know what to expect, or what was next but I knew it was going to be a journey.

God had called me and I accepted the invitation. The church in which God had placed me was a modern-day potter's house; God was shaping and molding this marred clay. It was here that I began to learn about the gifts of the Holy Spirit and see them in operation. It took time. It took trust. Also, it took patience to discern the voice of God and to trust in what I was hearing, even when it seemed radical.

God will utilize every moment of your life for his purpose. The experiences of life can become your great teacher or your greatest hindrance. I want to emphasize the importance of learning from your losses. When you face defeat, it's like experiencing two losses in one. The first loss is the actual event or situation that didn't turn out in your favor. The second loss happens when you don't take the opportunity to learn from that experience.

Imagine you're starting something for the first time. You encounter a difficulty where you keep failing and losing. If you just keep repeating the same mistakes without trying to understand what went wrong and how you can improve, you're missing out on a valuable chance to grow. By not learning from your losses, you're essentially losing twice.

The truth is, your life's journey shapes you in ways you can't fully control. Life throws unexpected challenges your way without warning. However, deep within you, there's a unique blend of qualities and strengths that are like the DNA of God, helping you overcome whatever comes your way. It's this inner strength that prepares you to face and conquer obstacles regardless of how life molds you.

CHAPTER 2

# I Look Crazy But I'm Better

**Here is another truth:** God has a plan for each of us. There are a billion plus people on the earth and no one's voice or fingerprints are the same, *no one's*! That is mind-blowing. We can imitate someone, we can duplicate them, however, there will always be something distinct about the original that the duplicate doesn't have. God is the greatest creative we have. He is masterful in individualization. It is this very individualization that God uses in your becoming to change and develop you. This undergoing is your becoming a better you.

People will not always see what you are becoming. Furthermore, what we are becoming doesn't always feel good because there is no blueprint of what we are becoming. People will not always see what you are becoming when God's hands are on you - your shape is taking place.

For example, let's look at the life cycle of the frog. The frog starts off as a tadpole until he hops out the water. The water is the container until he develops.  He will die if pulled out of the water prematurely. If a developing tadpole is removed from the water prematurely, it is unlikely to survive. Water is essential for its development and survival. They rely on it for respiration, hydration, and maintaining their body temperature. This aquatic environment provides all the necessary nutrients and it supports the whole process of this frog during its early  tadpole stages of life. The other tadpoles cannot see this whole process. They may sense that bits and pieces of their body are changing but yet do not fully know what's happening to them while they are in the same body of water.

The same happens to us when we are becoming.

Remember we are authentic. Each of us has an assignment and a calling. This gifting separates us from everybody else even though we may be in the same arena doing the same stuff. There was something special that you and I brought to the table that the other person cannot bring. God designed me to bring that degree of influence, power, and strength that couldn't be brought by anyone else but me. Every time God is about to catapult you into something major, He does three things. I know for sure:

He separates you

He stretches you

He shapes and builds you for the assignment

Why? Because, the process is needed and growth is movement. And it's okay if you're feeling uncertain because there's no visible blueprint for your future, remember that you're unique and genuine. Now of course we all have plans that we desire but they're not always what God has 'purposed' for us. Each of us has a special purpose and calling in life. We have gifts that make us different, even if we're doing similar things as others.

When God is preparing you, he separates you from certain things or people that might hold you back. Then, He challenges you to grow and expand beyond your comfort zone. And finally, He shapes and prepares you for the specific task ahead.

Why does God do all this? It's because He wants to use us to make an impact in the world. He doesn't want to hide our greatness but wants to empower us to shine and impact others. So, even if there's no clear plan, trust that by being true to yourself and relying on God's guidance, you can navigate your journey with purpose and confidence. It is God's desire to use us as agents of change. His plan is never to make you great and hide your greatness in the bushes. Here's what scriptures say:

*"Ye are the light of the world. A city that is set on a hill cannot be hidden. Neither do men light a candle, and put it under a bushel, but on a candlestick; and it giveth light unto all that are in the house. Let your light so shine before men, that they may see your good works, and glorify your Father which is in heaven."*
*(Matt 5:14-16 KJV)*

My potter's experience was a process that most people don't finish and usually run from. The time spent under my pastor's guidance was sixteen years, nine of them as a youth pastor. The process is never easy and sometimes we don't even realize the depth of the processing we have gone through until we get to a divine destination, a pit stop. This process is likened to the formation of clay by potters, which is quite interesting. Throwing is one of the first techniques and it is when the potter throws the clay into the center of the wheel to knock out or press out as many lumps from the clay as the potter can. It was the same way during the season of my process. I felt just like that clay being thrown into this thing called Christianity and not knowing what to do or how to move. It was awkward.

Many feel the force of the 'throw' when they accept Jesus as Lord and Savior and are unsure how to grasp the 'leaning into' the call of God. For clarity's sake, 'thrown' does not signify you were in unawareness nor that you didn't make the decision to be here, present to the call. It does acknowledge that you know this place you're in is new. Many of us feel 'thrown' with what we believe we are destined to do. Leaps of faith and new steps in major directions are those 'thrown' moments. You got this and you are feeling your own way through.

We are 'thrown' into business, into marriage, into careers, and into ministry. Here's the thing though, you being 'thrown into' is the kicker. It is the wheel the potter puts the clay on to start spinning. If you will, we are all 'thrown' and if that wasn't enough now we are all spinning, together on the potter's wheel - in the center of the wheel getting those lumps pressed out or knocked out. This is hilarious to me now, but early in life, it wasn't. I was clueless about God's plan for me. I can promise you things will look and feel like it's "out of nowhere" as if you have just been beamed into the twilight zone. If you don't know what I mean about the twilight zone, go look it up. Google it!

When the potters 'throw' the clay, it is done! They have removed as many lumps from the clay as possible so it can be made smooth to use. The clay must be smooth enough for the potter to be able to start the formation.

We hear a lot of people talk about the process yet everyone's process is different. I understand that. The purpose is all the same, it is to get us to a place where we flourish and stand solid in our divine place. For me, it wasn't the being 'thrown' that got me, it was the spinning. We all know we need help, there is no question about that. However, the part that stays in that divine place requires the spin. Yep, God is about to spin the block on you. No, that was a joke. Each of us have been in a situation that we had no control over. Absolutely none, no control. All we know is if God does not do *this*, it's over - the proclivities, life experiences, divorce, death, losses, and failed businesses.

Spinning represents a place of separation, or a place of exclusivity. This force of spinning takes you out of control of certain aspects of your journey. What I'm saying is that you lose the ability to control some things when God has you on the wheel, being made in the spinning. It will force the clay to start taking shape and expand when it's pressed and smoothed by the potter's hand. Some connections, even good people, are lost and normalcy is disrupted when the spinning kicks in. We all want to be great but must understand that loss and disruption is part of the next-level process.

I lost a good friend, Ronald, in the spin. He died of colon cancer. I remember going to visit him and the uncertainty of living was in his eyes. My friend was at times doubtful about surviving cancer, yet, Ron would always say, "I am in God's hands".

One Sunday, after church, I went by to visit him and he had tubes in his body around his stomach. It was terrible. We cried and prayed. I couldn't believe this was happening again. Someone close to me was going to die. Would I have the same bitterness I overcame from when my sister was murdered?

I loved this guy. He was always optimistic about everything and was a good friend to my wife and I. He introduced me to the IT world and loved helping people. He loved my family yet he died the very day my youngest son was born. Spinning is all I can say to explain why this was happening again. The spinning on the wheel of life again removes some things from your control. I was spinning. In one moment my wife was being rushed to the Hospital to have our son and in the next moment, my best friend Ron died. There was absolutely nothing I could do or even say. How do I handle this? Watching my wife rejoice our son's birth and also mourn for our good friend who died? "Make this make sense", was the thought that ran in my mind.

This experience held great significance for me as it coincided with my shared birthday with my sister, who tragically passed away in a heartbreaking incident. Every time I would celebrate my birthday I would have to remember my sister. It was difficult for many years to enjoy that day, or any day for that matter, but I finally got to a place where I could. Ron's death, on my son's birthday, is a constant reminder that *that's* the day Ron exited this Earth and that's the day my son entered this world.

Crazy, huh?

Nevertheless, by the grace of God, I didn't lose my mind or lose hope in God. I had all kinds of mixed emotions: grief one minute, joy the next. I felt the sting of being friendless one minute and then next again a moment of joy.

I wanted to rejoice because my son was here but then I received the news Ron was gone to be with the Lord; it was overwhelming. Ron had two kids that he would never get to see become men. It hurt just thinking about it. These were one of his many concerns that we often prayed and talked about. Rest in peace, Ron.

Wow! Life was full of transitions, turns, bends, highs, and lows. I understood that a leap of faith would be required in the throwing process. Also that losing important people, moments, and things was a part of that too.

Listen to Jesus as he responded to the crowd knowing they weren't ready for a real walk with him.

*"And there went great multitudes with him: and he turned, and said unto them, If any man come to me, and hate not his father, and mother, and wife, and children, and brethren, and sisters, yea, and his own life also, he cannot be my disciple. And whosoever doth not bear his cross, and come after me, cannot be my disciple."*
*(Luke 14:25-27 KJV)*

Some of our top motivational speakers have repeated things like this but the truth is Jesus said it first. There must be a sacrifice that you will endure if you're going to go up. There will be a God moment when you have to give up something that you hold dear to.

There isn't a next level in greatness or your calling without paying a price. This price may cost you blood, sweat, and tears.

The spinning causes you to be shaped by the hands of the potter in your abilities, rationale, knowledge, faith, and grace. This process stretches you.

What does that look like?

As I searched for ways to explain this, I remembered a ride at the state fair. This ride just spins you in a circle. The conductors of the ride don't buckle you down, you just spin around at such a force that you get stuck to the wall. While you are on the wall, the floor drops. The force of the spin gets so powerful that nothing in the middle can stay in position; it is held together by the force of the spinning. What is so amazing is that even though the floor has dropped you can't fall. Why? The force of the spin keeps you in place.

The people on the ride with me began to scream when the floor dropped. We are so accustomed to being in control that when things drop out of our life and when things unexpectedly disappear we resort and respond by screaming, crying, and wondering why it's happening. It's happening because - if we are going to do this, and if we are going to follow God, and if we are going to go after our dreams then, we will experience things that will be beyond our control. Things that will challenge your faith. We have to be willing to let God process our journey.

*"Then I went down to the potter's house, and, behold, he wrought a work on the wheels. And the vessel that he made of clay was marred in the hand of the Potter: so he made it again another vessel, as seemed good to the potter to make it." (Jeremiah 18: 3-4 KJV)*

Countless years of my life, I know, were spent on the wheel being pressed and spun. I am sure, even now, I am *still* on the wheel. I have not arrived but the ship has left the dock. Throughout those countless years, I can confidently say that I was constantly under pressure and undergoing a transformative process. Although we may not fully grasp the extent of our personal growth, both you and I are evolving. I made my way to a place called The Potter's House. It's a sanctuary for those who have experienced hardships which many of you are familiar with and yeah, I understand that you've heard the word processing so frequently that you've grown weary of it as well. However, each and every one of us must go through this processing if we want to thrive in life. People from all walks are currently on their own journeys in the Potter's House, a place of marred people whom God has chosen.

So many questions filled my head, as I am sure so many questions have filled yours like, "Am I headed in the right direction?" Because it feels uncomfortable, doubt pulls at us. I questioned myself so many times too. "Why am I here?" Again, that doubt can pull us into a deep abyss that some never get out of. So many walk around feeling like, "I don't fit in." Or "I feel awkward." Like I said, many times asking, "Why am I here?"

I don't understand what happened as I was learning who God was but I was stretched and was spinning.

**Signs that you're In the spinning stage**

1. When what we thought we had control of is lost
2. When what was familiar to us becomes unfamiliar
3. When things, people, and careers you fully trusted falls away
4. When you lose people close to you for no reason at all.

"With all of this that I had experienced, what now?"

"What did I do?"

I got to a place in my walk in life that I was tired of just enough: just enough peace, just enough faith, and just enough resources. It was as if I prayed for something like peace, it would last a week, then turmoil would strike again. I wanted to have it for just more than a week or a day. I was at my wits end because "just enough" wasn't cutting it anymore. I knew there had to be more. The truth is when you're constantly looking for more - more friends, more money, more love, more faith etc. - in actuality you're saying, "There has to be more to life than this."

When you've had a few accomplishments and you've conquered a few hills and valleys, but something in you is not satisfied with where you are then something is missing. This something is not being fulfilled by your career, relationship, finances, or connections. I will go further: you can be in a crowded room with friends and family but still feel alone and out of touch. There is this longing for something more that people, places, and things can not fulfill.

I can remember this for myself so vividly. I would try to connect with others. It lasted for a moment then something would happen that caused me to lose the connection. Most of the time when people discovered I love Jesus, it was as if they'd immediately change on me. It's like the GPS kept rerouting me, adding more distance and creating a bigger gap in time to the destination. Don't get me wrong I have established great relationships. Some people have even become like family, however I thought being connected to *someone* would help. It didn't fill the void. Do you know what was needed? A more intimate relationship with God.

We all need a more intimate relationship with God. That's the answer to the emptiness and discontentment you feel in your life. No matter how much you search, you will not find these missing pieces to the puzzle of your life in possessions. Neither will it be found in just attending church, regardless if you participated in all the activities. Many of you, thought you knew, how to go through all the esthetics and do all the church stuff to fill that empty space, yet the missing puzzle piece still remains. It can only be filled by a more intimate relationship with God.

Sometimes, you can get tired of attending church but don't stop going if it's fruitful and has helped you. This is the frustration of growing pains and the process. We can sense that there is more to God than just material things and church. We can feel that there's more, another step but grasping it is challenging. This brings me to another strategy of the potter after you are thrown and spun, he centers you.

The potter takes his thumb and puts it in the center of the clay until the clay is centered on the wheel. Check this out, you get centered while spinning. Even though things may seem out of tune and it may look a bit off, however, the truth is you are being put *into* alignment. God wants us positioned in the center of His Will not the w-h-e-e-l, but the W-I-L-L.

*"One of the biggest questions is not, What is my purpose for my life? But, What is God's purpose for my life?"*
*C.S. Lewis*

There are many things that *almost* pulled me out of the Will of God. One I will never forget is when I was offered to do a drug drop with a friend I met in church. I was struggling badly financially in my life and I was no longer able to make money like I was making it before. I will just leave it at that. Anyway, this gentleman came to me and said, "Man, I trust you and I know you're going through a tough time".

My response was, "Boy don't you know it. I need money more than a hog needs slop"

He went on to say, "I have a load I can pick up and I want you to go with me to make this money."

With excitement, I said, "Let's do it."

"We don't have to touch it", he said, "All we gotta do is park it and leave." This was my cue that it was something illegal.

"What did you say to me?" I asked him in shock. We had become close. I knew that he knew I was serious about God, but he also knew my struggles. I remember I said the dumbest thing ever. I said, "Man, I gotta pray about that".

As I think about it now it's hilarious but that moment was serious to me then. I had a relatively young family that was struggling financially. What's even dumber is that I did pray and God answered me. I wish this was a text message, instead of a book. I would drop some laughing emojis. Also, I would be lying if I said I wasn't ready to ride and get that money. I won't disclose the amount but it was enough to make anyone struggling, think twice. Nevertheless, the Lord told me if I left to go to Texas for the drop I wouldn't make it back. Long story short, I told him I couldn't do it and I told him what God said. I decided not to do it. Years later, it was my friend who ended up in prison. I believe without a shadow of a doubt that my friend still has a calling for ministry in his life.

Please hear me, God will allow you to do your own thing even if it's not His thing. He has given us the ability to choose whatever it is we want to do. However, there will *always* be something missing in that place if we choose it over what God has better for us, in the place he has chosen for us to be. See the potter takes his thumb and presses the clay in the very center of the wheel until a foundation can be formed for the specific pot that the potter is about to make. Sometimes the center of the wheel doesn't feel like the center of the Will. We think that the Will of God for our life comes with ease, peace, and joy. However that's not always the case, ask Jesus, ask Moses, ask Paul, and Joseph in the bible. Their stories are connected to crosses, jails, shipwrecks, pits, and wildernesses. I hate to say it but I agree. The safest place to be *is* in the Will and on the wheel of the potter.

**Signs you are being centered in the Will of God.**

1.  You feel something is missing, even in God.
2.  You sense a greater presence to seek God.
3.  You will encounter major distractions to disrupt the Will of God. But please know God has made a way out for it. (1 Corinthians 10:13)
4.  You will experience a level of being unsatisfied with life's routine.

Only God knows the things you've put up with and endured in the various stages of your life. God knows how much you've suffered, even though you did the right thing, and it seems you got the wrong outcome. At one point and time, you would curse folk and go backwards but the throwing and spinning helped you. You would have lost it but now you have come to a place in your life where you have realized you have wasted too much time, energy, and money on pleasing people. In fact, you have given people too much power!

God is saying you have exhausted your strength in the wrong place. You have reconnected with people hoping they would see what's missing and hoping they would help you. Let me make an announcement that you are really looking for you, not people. You are looking for the you that God designed and you're perplexed because you can not find it. Trust me, you have what it takes and God's process will soon reveal that to you.

Another interesting thing about the potter is that when he's designing the pot he uses water. Water makes the clay soft. Water causes the clay to be flexible and moldable in the hands of the potter. Water, biblically speaking, points to a few things: purity, power, deliverance, and the Spirit of God. The frustration isn't because you don't know God, it is because you're in His hands and you want whatever He is doing to be over with, quickly. Think about the frustration of Joseph. He was in jail for a crime he didn't commit and then forgotten about by people he had helped. I am sure it was frustrating knowing what God promised him but not seeing it yet, not as quickly as he would have wanted and also knowing he could not do whatever he wanted to do.

I have watched the potter's process. With every spin, he puts his hand into the bowl of water and brings it back to the clay. Without adding water, the clay will become hardened and tougher to mold. You and I are words spoken into existence by God. He doesn't want to control you only that you would love him enough to trust him with what he's doing to mold you and make you flexible to His Will.

*Isaiah 55:11 (KJV) says, "So shall my word be that goeth forth out of my mouth: it shall not return unto me void, but it shall accomplish that which I please, and it shall prosper in the thing whereto I sent it".*

Everyone that God has created has a Word within them that God has sent and that same Word that God has put within you, that was sent from Him, is meant to send you somewhere. However, many will not be sent because the elevated place isn't desired above all things.

The potter's work is purposeful and strategic. There were times in my walk with God where I did not desire the next level. It seemed as if the level or the experience I was having was tough enough. The very thought of going deeper or higher made me cringe. I retreated to my job, filling my days up with just doing work, hoping that this feeling of missing something would disappear, but it didn't.

This brings me to this: the potter keeps one of his hands inside the center of the clay. Then he brings the other hand to the side of the clay to form a wall or the body of the pot. The wall represents boundaries and protection. Boundaries are when God wants you to focus on your character and it's your character that is of the utmost importance. If you are a CEO, educator, politician, athlete, or pastor your character is what sets you apart. God knows that when the product is in the vase or the pot it must be solid enough and strong enough to hold the contents inside. If there is a crack in the wall of the pot the insides will soon be compromised. Look at athletes like Antonio Brown, an amazing athlete but his bad character tainted his gift. No NFL team will touch him because his bad character overshadowed things he did so well. I pray he bounces back and becomes a pillar of encouragement in society. While it is ultimately up to Antonio Brown to make positive changes in his life, our prayers and hopes for his transformation are meaningful gestures. They reflect our belief in the potential for growth and the possibility of a renewed character that can positively impact both the individual and society.

Remember Moses' one bad character lapse? It caused his own people to reject him. Proverbs 16:9 (KJV) says, *"A man's heart deviseth his way: but the Lord directeth his steps."* You may have a way you want to go but you need the Lord to direct your steps. Did you know that Moses knew what he was called to do before he even killed that Egyptian? He said in the book of Acts that he thought they would appreciate him more because they had seen the hand of the Lord was on him. That's found in the New Testament. Moses knew that God's hand was on him. Also, Moses didn't have a speech impediment. The Bible talks about how Moses was trained in all the ways of the Egyptians; he understood the language and he also understood all of the ways of how they lived.

Now, along the way while he was in the desert for forty years, Moses may have lost some of those things culturally and some of those behaviors. As with the potter forming the wall of the pot, building its boundaries and protection, so is Moses' life. God had stripped some things away because when he killed the Egyptian, he couldn't come back to Egypt looking the same. Moses had to come back looking like the delivered servant God had already seen in him before he became. During his time in the desert and in the wilderness, God formed him exactly how he wanted to make him. God wouldn't allow Moses to go back to the ways of the Egyptians or do the work in the ways of the Egyptians. I believe if God didn't strip Moses and formed him in that desert for forty years that the Israelites wouldn't have listened. Why? Because he, Moses, still looked too similar, looked too much like their oppressors. I remember when I had a few character issues that caused my ministry to be put on hold. At first, I felt that my character and my behavior was okay and justifiable but it was wrong on all accounts. The changes I had to make, like Moses, needed to stand out and identify me as different just like the process Moses went through formed him to be separate and prepared him to do God's Will.

**The process we have covered so far are:**
- **Thrown**- the beginning of separation and preparation.

- **Spinning**- the force that keeps you grounded and where things will be added and subtracted, that you have no control over.
- **Centering**- when God woos you into His Will and clues of the Will are discovered for you.
- **Shaping**- when God creates and forms you into something new in which character is paramount above all things.

There is an episode in our life after the shaping which we all have experienced that drives most of us crazy. It's called 'setting and waiting'. After all those tests, the first four tests, and all the trying, you would think that would be it. But no! You'll come into a season - into a place - of just 'setting and waiting' on God. Waiting on the right timing to execute what you know in your heart God has called you for. Waiting isn't the time you just sit and look around; it's the time you get to see what you can put your hands to do. God is observing. He is not learning anything new but you are. You are learning, so you can discover who you are after the throw, after the spinning, after the centering and after the shaping.

When I taught my daughter how to ride a bike it had training wheels on it. The training wheels on her bike served as a tool to help my daughter learn important skills such as balance, control, distance, and speed. They provided stability and support, allowing her to build confidence and gradually develop her biking abilities. When I felt she was good enough to ride on her own I took off those training wheels, gave her a push and watched. My daughter became more comfortable and proficient with her riding. If she fell during this learning process, I would rush as a caring father, quickly pick her up, wipe away the tears, and encourage her to try again. I think you get it.

There is no secret within us. We know our likes, dislikes, faults, and proclivities. He will use these moments to bring those things to the surface. Serving in ministries or a local church normally brings out who you are because it is a selfless act.

If you're under someone's leadership in ministry or a marketplace, serve with passion. Help with joy. I served in the marketplace as a negotiator and steward and oversaw contract negotiations. I didn't start out just leading straight out of the gates but there was a period where I had to learn to sit under someone as an assistant in order to acquire the skill set to do the job. Little did I know that the servitude I was rendering would eventually help me in ministry and business. The greatest joy in my waiting period or setting season was serving my pastor. I would look for ways to help in any way I could. I worked as a Sunday school teacher, sound man, janitor at times, and later, youth pastor.

*"Life's most persistent and urgent question is what are you doing for others." Martin Luther King*

During my time of sitting I prayed for the man of God, for the ministry, and served in every capacity that I was afforded. I had no hidden agenda but just to serve. There were times I wanted to preach but couldn't preach and I never complained. I waited. I didn't know what God was doing, until later - preparing me to be a leader of men and women. God knows the ending from the beginning. His intelligence is beyond our finite minds. He knows what he is doing. The potter lets the vessel he made sit to settle, to see if what he made holds up without any hands holding it in place. If you handle the wait, you are ready for the next process.

The fire may seem last but it's not. Fire fortifies what the potter made and in the setting, fire removes impurities. Fire strengthens the vessel that the pot is made of. I experienced some gut-wrenching things between 2008 - 2015 that made me stay before God. First was the passing of my grandfather in a car accident. Not only did my grandfather die in the accident but in the car with him were my uncle and his nephew. All died. If that wasn't enough, two years later my grandmother passed. She helped raise me; if I wasn't at home, I was with my grandmother. I loved my grandparents dearly. I learned how to slop hogs, feed chickens, and tend the garden with my grandparents. When I became an adult, I would often bring my grandmother to stay with me and she loved cooking homemade breakfast for my family. I thanked God for her life and what she deposited in me.

If that wasn't enough, my brother, Major, died after being ill. I remember walking into the room fifteen minutes after he took his last breath. I recalled the weight I felt, the heaviness and grief as if it was a cloud over my head. If *that* wasn't enough, a week later as we prepared for Major's funeral, my nephew, Major's son Terrance, came to town to bury his father. While he was here in town, he took his father's car to get washed. A day before the funeral, Terrance got robbed, shot at the car wash, and later died that night in the hospital. I remember walking into the room after the medical staff finished to confirm with the family that he was gone. Terrance's body was lifeless laying there on the gurney. His eyes were opened and all these tubes were coming out of his mouth. I was the minister and everyone at that time looked for me to be strong but I was the weakest I had ever been. I didn't know it but God was holding me up.

If *that* wasn't enough, my sister-in-law was diagnosed with cancer. My wife and I walked with her through the sickness. Then six months later, she died leaving behind four young boys. The Lord had said to me, "Jameson, there are angels in the room". I remember my sister-in-law telling me during a hospital visit she saw angels in her room, two of them. I eulogized her, but I had yet to mourn her. My wife during this time had fallen into depression. It seemed as if my house was in chaos. However, before the cancer, I was losing everything and filed for bankruptcy. Two years after that, God told me I was going to pastor a church. I have never in my life heard of anyone in my family starting a church from the ground up. I know. I know. It sounds crazy, but it's God. God uses everything we experience in life to help us be better. The paint, the colors, and the tapestry is decor that is put on the vessel that is decorated. Sort of like a soldier, we become decorated

41

because of the many accomplishments or battles we have overcome.

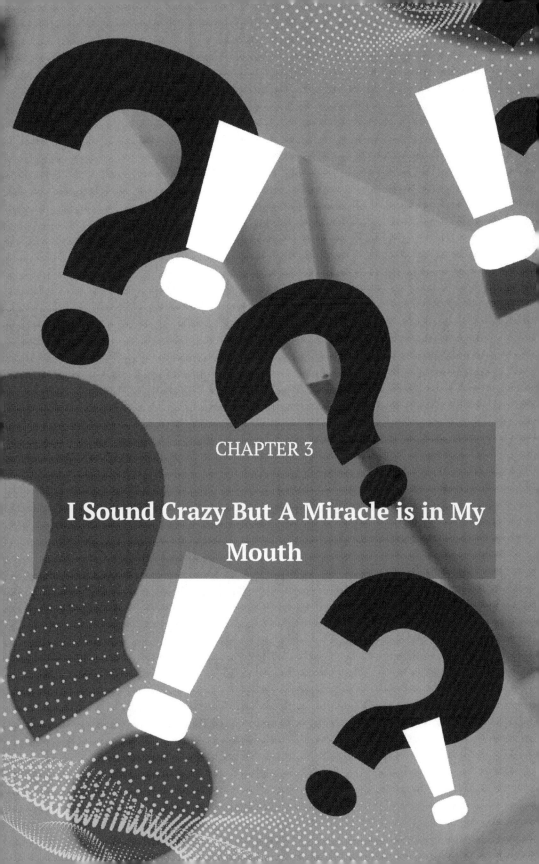

CHAPTER 3

I Sound Crazy But A Miracle is in My Mouth

On Palm Sunday, before I could preach, I felt the power of God moving in the room. I exhorted the people and encouraged them to praise God. While they were praising God. The Holy Spirit began to talk to me. I said to the congregation I don't know who you are but you came because you wanted to know if God was real. More specifically God said I'm going to show you I am real and on top of that I'm going to show up in your Mama's life. I didn't have a clue that someone had brought their Mama to the service to see if God would heal them. I had the musicians pause all the music. I declared to the church that the Lord had said, "He canceled cancer". Also, God said, "The person that had brought their mother came to be nosey and to see if the power of God was real". Then the Lord said to me to tell them, "Whoever it is, you came to be nosy but God said I am going to put my nose in *your* business".

The Spirit of the Lord said to me *again* to tell whoever it was, "Tell your Mama that the cancer has been canceled". The Lord then told me to say, "Whoever is in the room that has cancer come to me".

The daughter had brought her mother to the altar for me to pray for her. I began to ask the mother what was wrong. She told me that she had a tumor, a cancer on the left side of her head. I prayed, spoke to the cancer, and I told it, it was canceled and to disappear. Immediately the woman fell to the floor. A week later I got a text from one of the members of my church telling me that her mother's cancer had begun to shrink. The doctors had told her mother that this type of cancer doesn't shrink and normally carries a death sentence. Nevertheless, the power of God was working for that woman. A month later the mother who had the cancer reported that the doctor had removed her from all medications and treatment. The cancer was gone. Canceled.

Another powerful moment was when a young lady came to our service with tears in her eyes and she said that she hadn't been able to smell for two years. She wasn't able to smell after she had Covid-19. However, the Lord revealed to me that there were piercings that were in her lip and in her tongue with demonic ties to her issue as well. I said to her, "I'm going to ask you to do something that you may not like".

With her head tilted, she smiled and said, "ok".

Her husband was standing next to me with a look of concern, wondering what I was about to ask of her.

I told her, "Remove those piercings".

She smiled and said, "Okay, I will do it".

I asked, "You're sure?"

She said, "Yes!"

I looked at the husband and he was gesturing that it was ok. I said, "The reason I am asking you to do this is because the Holy Spirit said it was a demonic connection to the person (you) and your inability to smell".

She and her husband were quite shocked. Then the Lord instructed me to lay hands on her face and command her breathing and smell to be normal. Moments later that woman, who couldn't smell for two years because of Covid-19 and demonic ties had her sense of smell come back in two minutes. I can share countless miracles that have happened when I wasn't always confident and turned to God for His miracle-working power. I do understand that the same God that works in me, can work in you.

A miracle is a supernatural experience that cannot be explained by why or how it happens. For example, a woman who comes in with cancer goes to the doctor and a week later discovers the cancer is gone. That's a miracle! It's supernatural. Here is the truth: you and I are supernatural beings living in an earth suit called flesh. I know it sounds crazy but it's true. Again, you have God's DNA inside of you. One of the lessons in life I had to become aware of is that *everything* that comes out of my mouth will manifest according to what I believe. It is a consequence of my own thinking. If we think wrong, we will believe wrong. If our beliefs are wrong, our confessions will be wrong. In other words, what we say will be wrong. It all hinges on our thinking.

I want to be clear that this process never ends; it is never over until we die. We are constantly being decorated, designed and molded by the Father.

It's easy to think that after you've accomplished a few things and gone through a few things, that you are okay or that you are coming to the end of the process of being made. But God is constantly bringing us into a greater awareness of who he is in our lives by life experiences and everyday living. Bringing us to be mindful, alert to notice with the open eyes of awareness, like having a special relationship with a friend who you love very much. Every day, this friend does little things to show you how wonderful they are and how much they care about you. They might leave you little notes, help you with your homework or with your presentation, or travel the world with you, even plan huge events that get you to the next level. These things help you learn more about your friend and how they are always there for you. They show with action how they support you to your greatest and highest self.

In a similar way, many people believe that God is like that special friend. They think that God is always doing things to help us know Him better and understand how much He loves us. It could be through special moments we experience, like feeling happy or peaceful, or when things go well for us. It could also be through the love and kindness we see in other people, or the beautiful world around us.

People also believe that we can get to know God better by reading about Him in the bible, special study books, or listening to teachings about Him. We can talk to God through prayers, like having a conversation, asking Him for guidance or help. Sometimes, when we think about big questions or wonder about life, God can help us understand things better too. So, the idea is that God is always showing us who He is and how much He cares about us. It's like a journey of getting to know Him better and feeling His love in our lives. Just like you learn more about your special friend or an unknown person who does something kind for you consistently every day, people believe that God is constantly helping us learn more about Him too in that way.

Those challenges I had didn't break me but they did affect me. The key difference between challenges that affect you but don't break you and those that do is the ability to bounce back and continue moving forward. It is impossible to live in this world and not be affected by something or someone. When challenges don't break you, you find ways to adapt, learn, and grow from the experience. You may develop resilience, problem-solving skills, and a stronger sense of connecting to God. The challenges I faced left an impact and that fire didn't feel good but it made me appreciate life and also shook my faith a little.

I know I heard from God, but why didn't He hear me in those moments of trauma and pain? Why did bad things happen to good people? That was the lingering question that often troubled my mind. God was changing my mind again.

Changed minds will produce changed language. I often taught an exercise to bring my class into awareness. It was an ice breaker exercise within my classes that involved being asked to put our hand on our mind. While most people placed their hand on their forehead, considering it as their mind's location. I had a different understanding. I believed that the mind encompassed more than just the brain—it included the spirit and heart of a person. In my view, the brain is responsible for the body's functions, while the mind represents a deeper aspect of who I am.

During this activity, I had a realization. It felt as if God was showing me that my heart had been affected. I became aware of certain emotions or thoughts that were impacting my inner self and my feelings. It served as a reminder for me to pay attention to my inner man and recognize the influence it can have on my overall well-being. This experience highlighted the importance of nurturing my heart, understanding my emotions, and seeking growth in different aspects of myself.

*"For with the heart man believeth unto righteousness; and with the mouth confession is made unto salvation." (Romans 10:10 KJV)*

Whatever is in your heart is going to come out of your mouth. If you allow the throne of negativity to sit in your heart, your mouth will soon release it. Consequently, you will attract whatever you speak. Imagine that your heart is like a treasure box and whatever is inside that box will eventually come out. So, if you have good and positive things in your heart like: kindness, love, and happiness, those are the things that will come out when you speak. But if there are negative things in your heart like: anger, sadness, residue from trauma or mean thoughts, those are the things that will come out when you talk.

When you let negativity stay in your heart, it's like allowing a throne (a special seat) for those negative thoughts and feelings. And when they have a throne, they can control you and may cause you to say things that are not pleasant or helpful. This can make you feel dejected and attract more negativity into your life.

Sometimes even when you are helping others and doing good things, it can feel like everything has turned upside down in your life. You might feel like you are not receiving good things yourself. It's like you have been beaten up emotionally. It can be really tough and make your heart feel different, but remember, just because you are going through a difficult time doesn't mean that it will last forever. You are still able to help others and minister to them, even when you are facing your own challenges. And it's important to take care of your heart by filling it with positive things like: hope, courage, and gratitude. Eventually, things will get better and the negative feelings will start to fade away.

Everything was turned upside down in my life when my heart changed. Here I am ministering to people who are receiving miracles, blessings, and prophecies. Although I was beaten up I continued ministering.

Whether you believe it or not, the prophetic confession released from your lips will produce reality. The Holy Spirit is the driving force, the conduit of the prophetic and the baptism in the Holy Ghost awakens the prophetic within you. It produces the ability to call what is not into existence. However, it takes your commitment and connection with God to draw what's over in heaven for you into your reality. Also, that same mouth can draw hell into your reality altering your course. Let's be clear. Never underestimate the power of your words. They can bring life or death to you. If we, you and I, want to see a change in our life, we have to align our words with the word of God, not the situation.

There was so much turmoil happening in our life at one time that it seemed as if I would drown. Out of one thing into another. Buried one family member and then another. This scripture in Proverbs began to come alive in my wife and I.

*Proverbs 18:21 (KJV) states, "Death and life are in the power of the tongue: and they that love it shall eat the fruit thereof."*

We needed this Word because it seemed like we were on Groundhog Day. Have you ever seen the movie Groundhog Day? It depicted a guy in a virtual time warp, sometimes the same is in our life, it can feel like we are stuck in a similar situation over and over again, just like in the movie. Imagine waking up every day and it's the same day all over again, with the same things happening and no progress or change.

When I said it seemed like my wife and I "were on Groundhog Day," I meant just that. It felt like we were experiencing the same things and facing the same challenges repeatedly, without any improvement or new experiences. It made life feel a bit frustrating and had us feel a bit stuck. But the good news is that even when it feels like Groundhog Day, it doesn't mean that it will stay that way forever. Just like in the movie, the main character eventually found a way to break the cycle and move forward.

Your stomach will be filled with the fruit your mouth has produced. Let me say it this way: our words are like the ingredients that prepare the meal we will eventually consume. If we don't change what's on the menu, we will soon find ourselves consumed by the very words we have spoken, becoming full of ourselves. Our words have a big impact on how we feel inside and what will manifest because of our words. Just like the food we eat affects how our stomach feels, the things we say affect how we feel inside. If we keep releasing unpleasant things or being unkind we will soon have an unpleasant and unkind environment.

But guess what? We have the power to choose what kind of food (or words) we want to make and eat. If we notice that we have been saying unfruitful things or feeling discouraged, we can change that! We can learn new ways through the Word of God to speak to ourselves and others.

I went through a time when I realized this and learned an important lesson. I had to unlearn some old habits and ideas that were destroying me like a head on car collision. Then, I had to relearn new and better ways of thinking and speaking. It was like going through a stage of recalibration, where I was learning and growing. So, I want to share this with you because I believe it's important. Our words have power. They can affect how we feel and they can affect our future.

Change transforms your reality. There is life in your spirit that you must release out of your mouth. There is power in your voice. Our words are seeds. When we plant and continue to nourish them, they will grow. Whatever you speak continuously, whether its seeds of: power, lies, doubt, fear, pain, unbelief, hope, love, or care, those will grow and bear the fruit of your words. Sometimes we need a mouth-fast, that is, to spend less time talking. Examine yourself and what you are saying.

"What do you talk about?"

As believers, we need to change our language. Our talk should always rise above the level of the world around us. When you let the Word of God out of your mouth, it is not you speaking, rather, it's God's power literally stepping into your circumstances and changing them. Here are a few verses that shine a light on the power our mouth:

*"He that keepeth his mouth keepeth his life: but he that openeth wide his lips shall have destruction." (Proverbs 13:3 KJV)*

*"Let no corrupt communication proceed out of your mouth, but that which is good to the use of edifying, that it may minister grace unto the hearers." (Ephesians 4:29 KJV)*

*"Death and life are in the power of the tongue: and they that love it shall eat the fruit thereof." (Proverbs 18:21 KJV)*

Crazy circumstances and the adversary can't camp at your house or my house and... we won't know it. No, they have no power or permission. But, what the adversary will try to do is formulate a strategy that causes you to live in bondage. He does this by deception causing you to give him more power that he doesn't deserve. In fact, the devil, in my estimation, is responsible for only ten percent of your problem.

Let's not blame him! He has already been defeated. Look what happened to him at the cross:

*"And having spoiled principalities and powers, he made a shew of them openly, triumphing over them in it." (Colossians 2:15 KJV)*

Paul, the writer of this verse, is talking about Jesus' work against Lucifer - "And having spoiled principalities and powers, he made a shew of them openly..." Jesus stripped away the power the devil had over you. Colossians 2:15 talks about Jesus "spoiled". The word spoiled in this context is a military term used to describe what is done to soldiers who are captured in battle. As a Roman citizen, Paul used the terminology of warfare when he talked about how Jesus "spoiled principalities and powers".

When Rome fought against an enemy or a terrorist that threatened them, they would capture the leader. It is interesting to know how Paul painted a picture of what the enemy looked like after Jesus defeated him.

"What would the Roman Military do when they captured the enemy?"

They would cut his thumbs and big toes off, strip him naked, parade him through all the streets, and hook him up to the back of the chariot dragging him through the rest of the streets. Then all the citizens who were threatened by this enemy or were captured would all be gathered at the parade. And the families of those the enemy killed would watch and ridicule him. This was a parade for the people to celebrate and know that their enemy was defeated. Jesus said, "That's what I did to the devil for you. I cut his thumbs off. I made a public spectacle of him."

*"No weapon that is formed against thee shall prosper; and every tongue that shall rise against thee in judgment thou shalt condemn. This is the heritage of the servants of the Lord, and their righteousness is of me, saith the Lord." (Isaiah 54:17 KJV)*

In our own human strength, we cannot defeat the devil. However, Jesus took our place as a man, died on the cross, and rose from the dead, therefore having victory over sin and death. In doing so, He wrestled the power from the devil and gave it back to us.

Here is the problem: some of us have missed the parade. We don't know that the enemy has been defeated. We still have the same issues, we still have the same struggles, and we're still going through the same harassment.

But I say it again, *"The devil doesn't have any more power."*

The only reason he seems to be winning, even in brief moments, is that we have allowed a thumbless and toeless enemy to deceive us. We can't be afraid of a toothless lion. All that is left is his roar to terrify those who would fall for it.

In our own strength, as human beings, we are not able to defeat the devil. However, Jesus, who took our place as a human, died on the cross, and then rose from the dead. Through His death and resurrection, we gained victory over sin and death. This means that Jesus fought against the power of the devil, took that power away from him, and gave it back to us. The enemy you see now, you will never see again. The devil, who is often seen as an enemy, has been defeated by Jesus. But the problem is that some of us may not be aware of this victory. We missed the parade! We still face the same issues, struggles, and harassment in our lives which can make it seem like the devil is winning.

But I say it again, "*The devil doesn't have any more power*".

The reason it may seem like he is winning is that we have allowed him, as a toothless lion, to deceive us. We should not be afraid of a lion that has no teeth. The only thing left for the devil is his roar, which is meant to scare and deceive those who believe in it. Jesus has already defeated the power of the devil through His death and resurrection. We should not be deceived or scared by the devil's tactics because he no longer has any real power over us. Even though we may still face struggles, we can find comfort in knowing that the victory has already been won by Jesus.

*"Be sober, be vigilant; because your adversary the devil, as a roaring lion, walketh about, seeking whom he may devour"*.

*(1 Peter 5:8 KJV)*

All the devil can do is suggest and speak lies. And when you buy into that deception, that's when... you get snared. Remember David and Goliath? For forty days, the Bible tells us that all Goliath did was hurl insults and threats. For forty days, Israel's army was paralyzed by the sound and sight of this giant (*See I Samuel 17:8-11 KJV*). It wasn't until a lion showed up, in a person called David, to deal with a "toothless lion" that things changed. David refused to be disrespected and paralyzed by fear. David made the giant put some respect on God's name. David showed great courage and faith in God although Goliath the giant was feared. Everyone rumored of him as a powerful warrior who always challenged the Israelites. Everyone was afraid of him but David, a young shepherd boy, who stepped forward to face the giant.

David knew that with God by his side, he could defeat Goliath. He trusted in God's strength and protection. Instead of being scared or intimidated, David showed great respect for God and His name. He knew that God was with him and that he could rely on God's power to overcome any obstacle. With a single stone and a sling, David defeated Goliath. It was a remarkable and unexpected victory and teaches us that no matter how big or powerful our challenges may seem, with faith in God, we can overcome them.

It's like going to the doctor and they tell you that you have an incurable disease and you're going to die. That's the devil roaring!

You have to learn to roar back and fight back. He cannot defeat us, regardless of how bad it looks.

When I was a little boy, I used to love reading comics. I couldn't wait to get my hands on the latest edition of Superman. In some episodes, it looked like Superman was finished. The villain had overcome him and that was the end of him. Afraid to read any further, I would cautiously peek at the back of the book to know what happened in the end. My little heart would jump for joy when I found that my hero had turned the tables and spoiled the diabolical plans of his enemy.

I've looked in the Word of God to find out that in the end of our story, we win! You don't have to worry about whatever you're going through because at the end of the day, we too, can turn the pages to find out that we have the victory. No matter which way it goes.

*"Now thanks be unto God, which always causeth us to triumph in Christ, and maketh manifest the savour of his knowledge by us in every place." (2 Cor. 2:14 KJV)*

I know it looks bad. I know it looks rough. But, at the end of the story, you will come out on top. You will come out with power and with more confidence than you ever had . The story is not over! Yes, you should have lost it all. You should be frustrated. You deserve a gold medal, a purple heart, and a certificate for surviving the battle you've been through. You deserve an Oscar for smiling when you felt like crying. You have been through a lot but listen to these words:

*"Being confident of this very thing, that he which hath begun a good work in you will perform it until the day of Jesus Christ."*
*(Philippians 1:6 KJV)*

God is saying, "I will finish it. I will cause the finished product to manifest." Like in the comic book, there was a diabolical plan of the adversary to destroy Metropolis, yet Superman was the supernatural being on the Earth and stopped it. The pitiful pity party is over, blow out the candles on the sad little cake, and pop the balloons. God is supernatural and very real. This was exactly where I was. I had suffered so many losses that I didn't ever think that I could win. I was losing my house. We were losing our businesses. My children were going through personal battles and so was my marriage.

I remember working on my car in the garage and I broke down in tears. So much was happening. The saying coming out of my mouth was, "This is crazy!", so much so that it became my line, every time, "This is crazy!"

Two chapters ago, it didn't seem like God called me or was with me. My back was up against the wall so badly that I began to look like the paint. I had to even face losing my job because the enemy had started to attack me there too. All of the mental anguish, all of the heartaches that came my way was the enemy trying to break me but the potter had a plan to decorate and build me. So let me take a few moments just to encourage you, my friend. The lion, in you, is getting ready to get its roar back. You are built for it! You are getting ready to use your power and influence. You are getting ready to walk in your purpose, full of faith, when things seem to be falling apart. Get ready to roar!!

*"According as his divine power hath given unto us all things that pertain unto life and godliness, through the knowledge of him that hath called us to glory and virtue." (2 Peter 1:3 KJV)*

But, "Wait a minute. I'm broke. My family is in disarray. So how can Scripture say, "I have all things?" When I don't feel like I do. How can *I say* this, when I'm battling to keep my mind? I'm struggling to keep my job. The spouse has left; they even took the dog and the cat. Living from paycheck to paycheck."

Maybe it's true! Maybe you are living from paycheck to paycheck. I can remember a few times, I ran into a gas station as quickly as possible saying "Let me get $2 dollars on pump eight" and then ran out just as quickly because I was embarrassed. Whew, I know what it's like. True story: I know that if it weren't for the Lord, I would have lost it by now. I would have already quit.

Take heart, my friend. As you begin to grow in God and learn who He is in you, you will gain the knowledge of God. Your knowledge is tied to your thoughts and your thoughts dictate your actions. Those actions will soon produce results. When your thoughts change, the utterances of your mouth changes. If your head is in the right place, you don't have to worry about your feet.

What do I mean?

Wherever your head goes, your feet will follow. Think for a moment.

Where are you at this moment with God?

Wherever you are, it was your "thought life" that took you there.

As you continue to develop a relationship with God and learn about His nature and presence within you, you will grow into an understanding and knowledge of who He is. This knowledge is closely connected to your thoughts and your thoughts influence your actions. As your thoughts align with God's truth and goodness, your actions will naturally reflect that alignment. When your thoughts are transformed by God's truth, it will bring about a change in the words you speak. Your words have the power to shape your reality and affect the outcomes you experience. So, when your thoughts are in harmony with God's truth, your words will also reflect that alignment. This alignment of thoughts and words will ultimately guide your actions, leading to positive and fruitful results in your life.

Your mind and your heart play important roles in your spiritual journey. If you have a clear understanding of God and His ways, and if your thoughts are focused on His truth and goodness, your actions will naturally follow suit. Just as your feet follow the direction your head is facing, your actions will follow the alignment of your thoughts and beliefs.

So, it's important to consider where you currently stand in your relationship with God and your "thought life," which includes all thoughts and beliefs you hold. Together all brought you to this point.

My thought life contained my experiences of trauma, challenges, and significant changes in my life that deeply impacted the way I thought and perceived things. It was not always easy to talk about these difficult experiences. Yet, I believe it's important to open up and create understanding. At times I didn't know if I was going or coming. I had taken major falls that have embarrassed me and embarrassed my family. Yet, God was using that moment for *this* time to get me ready for the next phase of my life. Yeah, I know it sounds crazy but it's God. When God's hand is in it, you're going to be alright.

There's so much to tell you. I know I can't get it all but I will get as much of it as I can in this book, in this chapter. Let me share with you a revelation that seems simplistic but is absolutely powerful. The enemy is going to do his job and his job is to get in between your ears and mess up your mind. His job is to cause you to question whether or not God is with you. I shared with you that God spoke to me about these things. He showed me that when my knowledge is about Him that my mind will produce thoughts and results like Him. This will cause me to experience miracles like Jesus. God in that season changed me and I'm better for it. The

Bible said that God 'watches over His Word to perform it'. Jeremiah first chapter verse 12 says to me that the more Word I have in me, the more God will perform. He watches over his Word. He has to perform it.

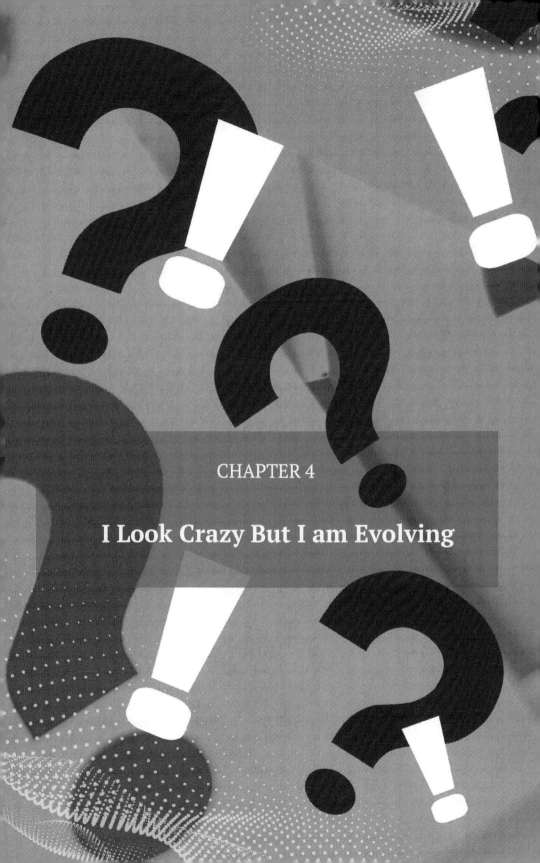

CHAPTER 4

**I Look Crazy But I am Evolving**

We were created so God would be glorified through our living on this Earth. The glory of God is His splendor, honor, favor, hand, power, and so much more. This same God placed his DNA inside of us so that you and I can do amazing things. I'm going to say this and you just might cringe. You and I can do amazing things without God. I'm not advocating to cut out God at all, but think about it. There are sensational men and women that have accomplished great things for centuries without even acknowledging God as the source - even though we have His DNA.

Thomas Andrews was the talented builder of the Titanic, a remarkable luxurious cruise ship that was considered unsinkable by many. However, instead of acknowledging God's role in his great accomplishment, Andrews said, "not even God can sink the Titanic". It was a statement of pride and overconfidence in human engineering. Well the ship, Titanic, sank and 1500 lives were lost.

This devastating event has served as a stark reminder of the consequences of arrogance and placing too much faith in human abilities alone, without recognizing the power and sovereignty of God.

The sinking of the Titanic is a powerful lesson on the limitations of human achievements and the importance of humility. It reminds us that no matter how great our accomplishments may seem, we should always acknowledge God's presence and recognize that our lives are ultimately in His hands. It's a reminder to approach our achievements with gratitude, humility, and a recognition of our dependence on a Higher Power.

Technology and mathematics provided us with tools and knowledge to unlock the mysteries of the world around us. They allowed us to delve into the complexities of nature and uncover its secrets. While many people, like Elon Musk, recognized the significance of mathematics in their work and appreciated its power, they have not viewed it through a spiritual lens or attributed it to a higher power. Elon Musk doesn't acknowledge God nor worship him, his "god" is technology.

In our journey of exploring and becoming aware, we encounter remarkable discoveries that shape our lives and society. Elon Musk is advancing our lives and society through that technology. However, it's important to note that not everyone sees these achievements like we do, like believers do, as evidence of a divine presence, evidence of God.

Another group, that can be found in Genesis chapter 11, that was doing great things but God wasn't involved were the people constructing a tower called Babel. They were together, in unity, and of one language, and of one mindset. They were focused and determined on building this Tower to reach Heaven. But here's something interesting, that God said in that same chapter, in verse number 6:

*"And the Lord said, Behold, the people are one, and they have all one language; and this they begin to do: and now nothing will be restrained from them, which they have imagined to do."*
*(Genesis 11:6 KJV)*

Wow, God himself acknowledges that we can do great things without him. Yet, I wouldn't want to do anything great and miss God. You *can be* great without God. *But, why would you* want to be great without God when you can *be greater* with God? Everything belongs to Him.

*"The earth is the Lord's, and the fulness thereof; the world, and they that dwell therein. For he hath founded it upon the seas, and established it upon the floods." (Psalms 24:1-2 KJV)*

You *can* accomplish much and *still* miss an eternal reward.

*"For what shall it profit a man, if he shall gain the whole world, and lose his own soul?" (Mark 8:36 KJV)*

Again, there is your strength, power, and influence and then there's God's strength, power, and influence. There is your idea and then there's God's idea. Our human strength, power, and influence is often fueled by our own ideas, our own accomplishments, and the resources at our disposal. We can come up with innovative ideas, create groundbreaking inventions, and exert influence over other people. However, when we compare our abilities to those of God, we realize that there is a vast difference. Huge!

God's strength, power, and influence are unparalleled. He is the source of all wisdom and knowledge, and His understanding surpasses anything we can comprehend. His power created the entire universe and sustains it. His influence extends to every aspect of our lives and beyond.

There is absolutely no question about it. We can't measure up to even an inkling of God's power to influence favor and grace. There is nothing wrong with trying to accomplish exceptional exploits but when we lose focus on where the ability came from that's when we're in disorder. There is something called anointing which comes from God then there is this thing called ambition which comes from us. It is built within us from God however there's a big difference between the two.

One is with God and with God's strength, an anointing which means to set someone apart, to authorize and equip him or her for a task of spiritual importance. The other is without God and with our own strength  is ambition which defines this desire to achieve a particular end, a determination for success. This is a powerful personal drive towards achieving goals which can be regarded as being of high importance to an individual. Often it is viewed negatively when these goals are selfish or evil.

There is nothing wrong with being ambitious unless it's applied to the wrong place. Ambition demonstrates an air that 'it's your strength not God's grace' and its ambition that questions, "What does the anointing have to do with this?"

When strength and Will run out the oil is still there. Why? Oil never spoils. I say this to mean God's grace and the anointing never ever loses its ability. Those of us who accepted Jesus are Priests and Kings unto God. The oil is a symbolic mark of the anointing that is smeared on us. Furthermore it is the sanctifying influence of the Holy Spirit upon those who are Priests and Kings unto God. Oil never spoils. The vessel (you and I) is what God has purposed for this Earth. It is never finished until it's over, through death. There are stages, graces, and times that will uncover you. It will evolve you if what you're doing involves ambition and anointing.

The transformation of caterpillars is intriguing. We all go through a period of transformation or evolving. When a caterpillar is born as an egg, it is normally on vegetation for most of its larva existence. When it becomes aware of its surroundings, it begins to feed on that vegetation - the very place where it was born. Similar to this caterpillar, we are born into environments that we quickly begin to absorb. Whether the environments are good, bad, ugly, or indifferent. We begin to absorb them, in the innermost parts of our being, it molds us. When we're 'born again' the culture of church and its teachings begin to be absorbed; it molds us.

Whatever we choose to digest becomes nourishment for us. We grow in similar ways just like how a caterpillar consumes food to fuel its growth and transformation. Our spiritual growth is nurtured through the consumption and internalization of God's Word. Whatever the caterpillar is eating has developed something in its stomach. Likewise, what we eat will develop in our stomach or spirit. Just as the caterpillar's diet influences its physical development, what we "feed" ourselves spiritually can impact our inner being or spirit. The Word begins to create some beautiful and powerful things as we begin to digest it or live it out, if you will. This beauty will then manifest on the outside to show others that God lives in you and is active in your life.

In the caterpillar's life it is the very thing that he eats that will create the very thing he needs for his next transformation, which will be going to come out of his mouth. The vegetation he has digested has become the silk being released from his mouth, within him, to form the cocoon. The caterpillar needs this for its next phase. That silent 'wow' factor in the stages of metamorphosis, the evolving and transforming. This is exactly what is happening in the life of the believer. Just like in the life cycle of the caterpillar, what the believer has been eating in their spirit, feeding their mind, and the words being spoken out of their mouths is going to eventually create transformation.

What have you been feeding on?

What's coming out of your mouth?

*"And be not conformed to this world: but be ye transformed by the renewing of your mind, that ye may prove what is that good, and acceptable, and perfect, will of God."  (Romans 12:2 KJV)*

After some time, when the caterpillar is well-fed and rounded, it begins to build this cocoon around itself.  This cocoon gets built by what's being released out of the caterpillar's mouth. After a few days, it struggles inside the cocoon. We see it in nature though as an "all of a sudden" thing, when it breaks out and through it. We don't see the totality of the inside struggle. We just know that it struggled on the inside and now it has transformed into this colorful beautiful butterfly that is no longer Earth-bound but is at liberty to fly for a season.

Every person that God has used to do sensational things had to evolve. Those individuals had to be transformed. There was a point in my own walk with God where I was "good" at things, but He was going to use those more difficult moments to build me up for the things to come. If we'll be honest, sometimes we know within ourselves, we need deliverance. But, we bury it because we know it requires more than what we're willing to pay for it. There is a price to pay in each of the stages of transformation. Think about it!

This caterpillar was once on the level of an ant, a beetle, and the worm. The only way that the caterpillar would stay on the same level as the insects or invertebrate I just mentioned, is if it never transforms. We all know life is full of levels, turns, challenges, changes, and transitions. Moses had to evolve into the deliverer. Abraham had to evolve from Abram to Abraham, a father of many nations. These destinies did not come about until they obeyed God, left the area and the environment that they grew up in. This move was pivotal for their transformation. Joseph evolved from being just a spoiled child to second-in-command in all of Egypt. The pit, the palace, the prison and all the moments in between were dedicated to his transformation.

There was a period in my life where I wanted to be what I saw in other prominent church leaders and what they did. I wanted to just travel and preach. During that time, I was very zealous and ambitious. I began to travel, doing revival, and preaching internationally. The Lord blessed me with a few businesses: a freight transportation company, real estate investment property and a home inspection business. I was very ambitious then, but after a while, my life began to shift. God permitted me to start losing everything, yet I didn't know it was God.

I had lost my house, my businesses, and almost my marriage. I had lost connections because I was so busy trying to pull together all the other things that were coming apart. Those relationships that I built, I could no longer focus on. I was being stripped! I was in, what I thought, was survival mode. However, it was God mode. He was about to use those moments to transform my life.

God mode. It's a cheat code. A code that gets us ready for destiny and transforms us. I was good with traveling, ministering the Word of God, coming back home, and serving my leader. I had no intentions of ever leaving that comfortable place. I was doing what I wanted to do. There I was good. Yet here I was, being very successful at it, but He (God) had another plan.

I knew something had changed. I went from a season of winning to a season of losing and losing badly. My wife and I did the best we could to survive in that season. One of the many tough moments that I remember was when my son played baseball and we had to take a trip out of town. We put our money together the best we could to get the hotel and for him to just have a good time. My entire family went with me including my oldest daughter and my oldest son. Every step of the way we watched every dime we spent. Our children had no idea the struggles we had faced, but I remembered. On our way back home, we had a little money left which we stopped to put what we had in gas, in the vehicle. It didn't move the needle much because it was still so close to empty. We prayed all the way down the road that we would make it home and wouldn't break down. God answered our prayers and we made it back safe and sound.

That season was a hard season, a difficult season. I took pride in taking care of my family, yet it felt like I was failing them. I experienced a lot of challenges and pressure. The pressure of that moment was producing in me a far greater glory than I was aware of. It was a tough time and I felt like everything was falling apart. In other words, the pressure was producing something in me that was necessary for my next level. No one besides my parents knew that we had lost everything at that moment. Only they knew the full extent of what we were going through. We had lost everything and it was a secret burden we carried.

The house I had built for my wife and promised her was in foreclosure. We lost the house. The house that me and my wife dreamed about and prayed about, we lost. God gave us our desires and now it was taken away. The house we testified about, shared with others, and claimed, as the blessing God gave us was gone.

While going through the season of losing, I was having flashbacks of every step of the process in building that home from the ground up. I remember taking my kids to view every stage and telling them, "Look what the Lord has done for your mom and I". They had no idea the turmoil that was going on. It felt like I was being stripped or punished or as if God had forgotten about me.

"Did I do something wrong or did I mess up?" Those kinds of thoughts kept flooding my mind every single week as we waited to see if the foreclosure was going to really happen or if God would come to our rescue.

Well, we lost the home.

"How was I going to explain this loss to my children, our family and my friends?"

I was embarrassed! It seemed as if I wasn't hearing the voice of God. The voice of my troubles was made louder than the voice of God. My focus had changed. I was like how can I hear the voice of God so clearly for others when now it's like He has me on pause. I had a clear sense of hearing God's voice when it came to guiding and helping others, but now, it felt like there was a silence in that communication with Him. Sometimes, our journey with God involves different seasons. There are times when we feel a strong connection and clarity in hearing His voice. And, there are other times when it may seem quieter or more challenging to discern His guidance.

Another hard lesson I learned is when I fell so hard that it landed me in jail. I just knew my ministry was over for sure. How could I be so stupid? This was my lowest. As I laid on that bunk in the cell, I just knew God was done with me. However in my unknowing, God was up to something major in my life. He was going to use every mess up, every failure, and every issue to decorate this vessel. I was feeling discouraged, disappointed and defeated yet this time of pause or silence, didn't mean that God had abandoned me or stopped speaking to me. Instead, it was an opportunity for me to deepen my trust in Him, to seek Him even more, and to grow stronger in faith.

Let me share that this very hard season and challenge is decorating the general in you. That you, that you will become, if you don't quit. Quitting is the language of losers and is the easy way out to answer our problems. When we quit, we deny ourselves the opportunity for growth, learning, and eventually success. Many successful people have faced setbacks and encountered difficulties along their journey, yet, what set them apart is their determination and refusal to quit, just like Elijah who felt defeated and forgotten when he found out that Jezebel wanted to kill him. Elijah, faced a moment of discouragement and desired to call it quits when he found himself engulfed with Jezebel's threats against his life.

Despite having his earlier victories and powerful experiences, Elijah still felt defeated and forgotten in that particular moment. Yet, what made Elijah's story remarkable is that he didn't allow his temporary discouragement to define his entire journey. Instead of giving up, he sought God's guidance and found strength to continue. In his moment of despair, God provided Elijah with sustenance, rest, and reassurance. Through an encounter with God, Elijah realized that he was not alone and that there were still important tasks ahead of him. He discovered that his purpose and calling were not finished, and he regained his determination to press on.

Elijah's story teaches us the importance of seeking God's presence and allowing His strength to sustain us during difficult times. It shows us that even when we feel defeated, and we may have forgotten God's promises because it has been such a long difficult season, that God has not forgotten us. He is always there, ready to renew our spirits, and remind us of our purpose.

Elijah was under a juniper tree depressed and wanted to die. He was so discouraged and thought he was the only prophet left in all of Israel. Elijah just like I did, thought God had forgotten. Nevertheless, God intervened, spoke to Elijah to assure him he was not Alone, and He (God) hadn't forgotten him.

*"And he said, Go forth, and stand upon the mount before the Lord. And, behold, the Lord passed by, and a great and strong wind rent the mountains, and break in pieces the rocks before the Lord; but the Lord was not in the wind: and after the wind an earthquake; but the Lord was not in the earthquake. And after the earthquake a fire; but the Lord was not in the fire: and after the fire a still small voice." (1 Kings 19:11-12 KJV).*

The enemy will use every strategy he has to prevent what God has promised you from being realized. He particularly wants to stop the words you have spoken from being manifested. But the devil is a liar. God will destroy every demonic roadblock, satanic voice, and negative word that has been spoken.

He says, "I am settling it now. I am releasing a voice in your ear for you to hear what I'm about to do with your life."

Your life has purpose written all over it.

Don't let the enemy rob you of the promise. God has prepared a table before you in the presence of your enemies. Let me announce that food resources, sustenance, energy, and strength are about to be served at the table. The Lord himself will speak as He did to Elijah. We may not hear His voice in the thunder, the earthquake, the shaking, and the breaking. Instead, He may speak to you in a still, small voice that says, "I got you".

Our trials will not last forever. God will blow your mind when He intervenes in your situations or shows you what's next. It will happen at a time you may not expect. We lost the house and we had approximately thirty days to find a new place to stay. We looked everywhere but because of our financial situation we were unable to get anything. The Lord knew what He was about to do. During this challenging time, our next-door neighbor faced a problem that led his wife to relocate to another state for a few years. As a result, they needed tenants to lease their house. Coincidentally, this situation aligned with our own desperate need for a place to stay, as we had lost our own house. It was a difficult moment when we had to approach our neighbors and share our situation with them. We were in a vulnerable position and needed their understanding and help. However, little did we know that the Lord was already working behind the scenes, orchestrating events to provide for us.

As God would have it, everything worked out so we moved into the house next door. I remembered when we just grabbed our clothes from the closets in our house and walked across the street where every neighbor could see us moving into the house next door. We dragged what we could from our house to their house. My children had to do the same. Going back and forth, we'd often drop some clothing in the street and would have to double back to pick up the clothes as people watched. I was so embarrassed and had no idea what God was doing.

Even though we had found another place to stay it was difficult that every day I came home to pass by the house that God had blessed me with. Hear me! The house was right next door in the cul-de-sac. My wife and I were heartbroken. My kids were confused as to how this had happened. My wife would have days that she would just cry as she passed by the house. Once she shared with me how she felt so defeated like we had failed as parents. That was so hard to hear her say but I felt the same way. It was as if I was watching God give my promise to someone else. I had to watch as others moved into a house God had given to me. My new neighbors never knew we ever owned that house at one time. That's crazy but it's God.

Trust God. He knows what he is doing to the vessel that He's making. One thing we were committed to was to never stop serving and giving to our church. I didn't want the enemy to win, period. I wasn't going to change my testimony or my stance. The power of evolving and transforming was never pretty. What *we* thought was the end was God releasing a new beginning for us. He did it at moments we least expected. I was comfortable in my "new normal". It seemed as though the very moment I started getting comfortable that was the very moment things started to unsettle.

God always does something that disturbs our comfortability. I'll never forget the moment I was at an ordination service, serving as a presider. While the service was going on, I heard the voice of the Lord. I was standing there looking at the program to see what was coming up next, when the Holy Ghost gave me utterances. No, I did not speak in tongues. Nor did I dance by the inspiration of the Holy Ghost. Neither was I in prayer when God spoke.

The voice of the Lord said these words, "You're going to pastor".

When I first heard them, I responded negatively. It was an immediate default reaction.

"The devil is a lie."

You must understand. I just got things back to *almost* normal and was still battling, mentally, what had happened to us.

The Lord repeated it again, "You are going to be a pastor".

I said, "Lord, a pastor? Are you sure?"

I know that's crazy asking God if he was sure, but I did.

"Lord, if I'm going to pastor", I inquired again, "What am I going to name the church?"

He said, "Bethlehem".

**Disclaimer:** I mean no offense ever to any religious organization or person. Please forgive me in advance, charge it to my head, not my heart.

I was in total shock. "Bethlehem?", I said, "God that sounds like some *old* Baptist Church in the woods somewhere". Still in disbelief, I continued inquiring, "Bethlehem?! Lord, isn't that the place where Jesus was born?"

"Yes", He said, "and Bethlehem will be the place I'll be born into the hearts of my people."

I didn't understand why God would want me to pastor, seeing that I'm just six to eight months out, maybe a little less out from bankruptcy, and all I have left is a little bit of money.

Pastoring a church was the furthest thing from my mind. I was barely getting back on my feet and heard God tell me, I'm going to pastor. I knew it was God, without a shadow of a doubt, but yet I kept what he said in my heart. At the time, I didn't even share it with my wife because it just seemed so far-fetched, so far out, and so far away from what I wanted to do. I spent the next two years seeking God about how I should do this. I had Gideon syndrome. I wanted to know just like Gideon did, about every move God wanted me to make. I was prayerful and careful. I wanted to be sure that this was God because I knew that it was a heavy responsibility. I didn't want a public failure like the private one I had. I was timid and afraid to move because of my failure last season. That was the real reason. I needed reassurance that this chapter wouldn't be like the last chapter.

I also knew that it would be hard for me to leave my church. I loved my church. I had to work up some courage to share with my wife that God was calling me to start a church. Mind you, that my wife earlier, in our walk with God, got too much care for me being a preacher. So I didn't know how she was going to take this. Let me be clear, she did *not* want a preacher for a husband. She just wanted her husband. Even in my calling, as a prophet of God, she loved me and supported me.

When I finally told my wife, Tomecka, it was as if she knew the whole time, and was waiting on me, to my surprise. She prayed for me and gave her full support, which was all I needed. I recall gathering my family into the living room to tell our children. I was so nervous because of what we just came out of, what we just struggled through. My confidence was not all there, nevertheless I told my children.

My daughter said to me, "Dad, it's about time!"

My two sons said, "We were wondering when you were going to do it".

I was so relieved yet I asked them if it would be a problem for them, after explaining all the sacrifices I would need to make.

They all said to me, "Dad, it's okay we know you're going to do good".

I had tears in my eyes because they still trusted their Dad, even after a major failure. Man, I got tears in my eyes right now, just telling you, as I read this myself on what happened.

From that moment things begin to shift. Everywhere I went for a year and a half, God was confirming what he spoke to me through people that didn't even know themselves, nor what God said to me. About a year and eight months in, I finally decided to tell my pastor. It was as if he already knew that God was calling me, too. He gave me strategies on what to do but we'll save that for my next book. Let's just say, I have honored those strategies from that day up until now.

I can recall a time when someone shared their thoughts on strategy with me on how I should prepare and launch the church or not do it, at all. When they shared their thoughts with me it gave me reasons to pause because I loved them and trusted their thoughts: "If you can, do plan A, which is to pastor and God will bless you. You can also do plan B, and that's to continue to evangelize, not pastor, and God will bless you".

Why am I sharing this part?

Why?

Because God is about to put his stamp of approval. His stamp on what he wants me to do, without question. The source was a very credible and reliable person that I believed in.

When Sunday came, I went to visit a church. The pastor knew me but he had no idea what God had said to me and what I was about to do. No one knew but a few people. Those few people had no clue I was going to church.

As soon as I walked through the door of the church and made my way to the pulpit, the pastor said to me, "Prophet, you need a Word from God".

Unbelievable, right?

Now remember, I had just gotten that Word of plan A and plan B from someone else, who was one of the trusted voices in my life. I was beginning to pause the move. I was sitting there listening to the man of God lay out His introduction for His message. The title of his message was: "The promise is Isaac, *not* Ishmael." Subtitle: "It's plan A, not plan B."

Wow, mind blowing! Absolutely...mind-blowing!

The hairs on my head stood up. I could feel the power of God radiating just in that statement alone. I know that sounds crazy, but it's God. I had no conversations with that man of God before or even after he finished preaching. I just knew then, I had to start moving. The following Sunday, I went to visit a friend's church to support them in their Pastoral Appreciation.

The man that my friend was renting the church from, *happened* to be there, at the pastoral celebration. I sat in the back. I mean all the way in the back, my wife and I. Just when they began getting ready to dismiss, the service man who owns the building and yet doesn't know me, points to me, and says, "Hey you in the back, with the black suit, with the black and white shirt. I don't know you but God is about to blow your mind with the ministry. I don't know if you started the ministry, yet but God wants you to know that he's with you."

I went, literally, into tears just remembering those moments because God knew what he wanted to do with me before I knew anything.

This was a new phase, a new era, and a new season that God was bringing me into. What is it? I couldn't tell you at the moment but things were manifesting. I would have never picked me. This new season the potter has for the clay will be sensational. It will be phenomenal and God will see us through it. This season will stir up faith. I know it's crazy having faith in a God we can't see, telling us to do something we have never done, with money we don't have. Man, I just filed for bankruptcy. On top of all that, no one is around to help. It looks crazy, but God is in it.

Faith is putting in action a plan to do, when we can't see it. We don't need faith when something you already see is manifested.

It is already there. No need to believe, when you know. Without a shadow of a doubt, you don't believe, you know it. We all exercise faith every day. We can't see sin. Neither do we know what a sin looks like, yet we believe all of our sins have been forgiven. We asked to be forgiven although we can't see the forgiveness. Even still, we walked around confident that we were forgiven. Think about that.

Something we can't see or touch is pure faith.

Did you see God take an eraser and wipe away all your sins?

No, but you believed the Word that God spoke. At this moment, all I have is a Word to do something. All you may have is a Word. That Word from God needs your attention and focus to manifest on this earth what God has deposited in your own thoughts and heart. I have never planted a church before. I don't have a blueprint. Nevertheless here we go.

CHAPTER 5

**You May Look Crazy But Start**

Lies and distractions will be the force that fights against you when plowing forward. Lies will bring you into constant conflict with the Word God has spoken over our lives. The devil is the father of lies. When you believe his lies, you are in *no* position to fully receive the things of God. It is critical that we maintain the right character and don't yield to distraction to bend us out of shape. Even a good thing, that is contrary to God's will for us, can contaminate us, making us something impure and unsuitable. When you are contaminated you come into contact with something unclean. Just because it's good doesn't mean God wants you there at the moment. Divine appointments are missed because we get distracted.

My flesh was fighting me every step of the way to plant this church. I was moving forward with a small team that I had assembled. Which I knew would no longer be with me in the coming weeks. As the days drew closer for me to launch out, doubt started to creep in, and thoughts of stopping were constant.

Was I making a mistake?

Was I moving too fast?

Why?

Why am I thinking all of this?

The fear of failure. Fear will make you rebel. If you rebel against the Word that God has given you, it's rejection. If you constantly reject God, inevitably, you will miss your divine destiny. I have learned that where **fear** is tolerated, faith will be contaminated. Fear will attempt to steal your focus however when intentional focus is present, nothing can stop you.

On March 15, 2015, the church was established and on March 22, 201, we had our launch services for the new church. I used the last bit of savings I had in my 401k to get everything started up for this church and when I finished I was down to nothing. My friends, my family, my former pastor, and the church came to send us off. My family and just four others were with me as we started the work of ministry. I had no idea on how things would work. We had our first official Sunday service the following Sunday. God didn't tell me to start it in my home or anything like that. He charged me to go out and find a place where we could start the ministry. That place was an old video store with a basement maybe about five hundred to seven hundred square feet.

It wasn't much but it was a start. It was a shared space. We would often have to wait until the church before us finished so we could start. One church would have services at 11a.m., and my time slot would be 3p.m. We would sit in the car and wait patiently until they finished their services before we would start. One of the things we noticed that was so interesting about this place is that behind the podium was a big cross. This cross had a nail at the foot of it. This nail was huge. Oftentimes during a Sunday morning message, if I backed up just a little bit, too far backwards, that nail that was sticking out from the cross - the head of that nail - would hit me in the back. I really don't know if the owner of the place designed it that way. Nevertheless it was a reminder. A reminder of two things: number one to stay humble and number two for a reminder of why I was there, because of Jesus. We did our best in that Ministry location. There were so many miracles that took place there, it was mind blowing.

Cancer was healed. There was a lady that couldn't walk. God touched her body and she didn't just walk, she ran. This is just to name a few. However, it was a great challenge doing the work of ministry. I often had to pay the rent out of my own pocket. Those were sacrifices that were made to help families in need, even though we didn't have it ourselves.

People came and they left. I don't know to this day why. Maybe it was because of the location. Maybe I wasn't big enough for them, yet. I remember one situation in particular. Listen closely to what I'm about to share. I remember this particular family, I won't call any names, that started out with me in the beginning. I'll never forget. I was at home, getting ready to watch television, and this was after coming out of prayer. As I began to turn on the television, the Lord spoke these words, "They are going to leave you."

I pause for a second. I couldn't believe that, but I knew I heard God. God said it again.

He said, "They are going to leave you, but it's not me doing it. It's them doing it. When they tell you it's me, tell them it's not, but they are free to go".

My heart sank and my feelings were hurt because it was hard for me to believe that they were going to leave. They were family. They were a critical part of the ministry and a great help.

*"And he said, Go forth, and stand upon the mount before the LORD. And, behold, the LORD passed by, and a great and strong wind rent the mountains, and brake in pieces the rocks before the LORD; but the LORD was not in the wind: and after the wind an earthquake; but the LORD was not in the earthquake: and after the earthquake a fire; but the LORD was not in the fire: and after the fire a still small voice." (1 Kings 19:11 KJV)*

So, I picked up the phone, we had a light conversation. I proceeded to ask the lady what God told them to do for the ministry. She told me, the Lord said to them that "they were to help me build this ministry".

My response was, "Wow, I'm really looking forward to the amazing adventures we will experience together."

We continued the conversation about other things and then I presented the same question. They responded with the same answer previously stated. They told me the Lord said to them that they were here to help me build this ministry. We talked about a strategy that we were going to implement to help market the ministry moving forward. Then I again, for the third time, asked the lady the same question, just like Jesus did when He asked

Peter to feed his sheep three times, "What did God tell you to do for this ministry?"

She responded on behalf of them with the same answer.

In the story of Jesus asking Peter to feed His sheep three times, we find profound lessons of forgiveness, restoration, responsibility, and service. After Peter had denied knowing Jesus three times, Jesus appeared to him and lovingly reinstated him. He asked Peter three times if he loved Him and commanded him to care for His followers, emphasizing the importance of tending to the spiritual needs of others. This interaction showcases Jesus' grace and second chances, while reminding us of our calling to extend love, compassion, and guidance to those around us. It serves as a powerful reminder of our role in nurturing and supporting others on their spiritual journeys.

The repetition of the question and of the command amplifies the significance of the message, emphasizing the depth of Jesus' love for us and the importance of our relationship with Him. It highlights that following Jesus involves not only personal faith but also a commitment to serve and care for others.

As I began to get off the phone, I said to the lady, "I want you to do me a favor".

She replied, "Sure, what is it?"

I said, "I want you to write this day down, the date, and keep it with you at all times. This day and date is going to be very critical for you in the future. It *will prove* to you, *something,* in the near future.

Two months later, the lady and her husband asked to see me after service. I was already aware of what was going to be said. I had prepared my wife, as well. I told my wife what the Lord revealed to me previously that they were going to leave. When we all went to the office, one of the wives said to my wife and I, that the Lord had told them to leave the ministry.

I asked both her and her husband, "Where are you going to go?

We don't know yet," They said. I noticed the wife had turned to look at her husband as she said it.

Keep in mind that the husband had no idea of the conversation his wife had with me on the phone two months ago. So I proceeded to tell her. "Do You Remember our conversation on such and such a day?

She said, "Yes, I remember".

"Do you have *that* day", "And *that* date, on you, right now?

She said, "Yes!", and proceeded to pull out the note she had written on that day and that date we had the conversation.

Then I dropped the bomb. I spoke to the wife and I said, "On that day and that date, was *the* day, God told me you were going to do this. Furthermore, you would also need to know the real answer as to why you both are leaving. The answer is, "God didn't tell you to do this, but you're free to go".

They were stunned and at a loss for words. The husband said out loud," Oh, wow!" as he looked at his wife in disbelief.

The husband almost fell out of his seat from the insight of God that was revealed in that moment. I wanted to say that this was not an opportunistic moment to cast a negative light on them but to maximize and reveal something major they needed to come to understand.

Family and friends will come with you on the journey. Some will leave because they can't see the vision or maybe they are looking for something bigger or better. They *may* come to help. You *may* be overjoyed. You *may* be excited. I wanted to caution you, however, that your help will not always come from those that are close to you. It may not even come from the people you trusted that will be there for you. Your help may come from the people you least expected. King David brothers didn't help him to be king. God used Jonathan, the son of King Saul, to instruct him in the ways of the king. Jonathan was a great friend to David.

*And Saul's son Jonathan went to David at Horesh and helped him find strength in God. "Don't be afraid," he said. "My father Saul will not lay a hand on you. You will be king over Israel, and I will be second to you. Even my father Saul knows this." The two of them made a covenant before the Lord. Then Jonathan went home, but David remained at Horesh. (1 Samuel 23:16-18 KJV)*

We see that God orchestrated a unique friendship between David and Jonathan, and we also see the ways in which God can use unexpected connections to bless, support us, and encourage us to reach our full potential. . Despite David's challenging circumstances and lack of support from his own family, God provided him with a faithful companion helping him navigate the path to kingship. It reminds us of the importance of true friendship and the ways in which God can use unexpected connections to bless, support us, and highlight the significance of having people in our lives who believe in us and encourage us to reach our full potential. Just as Jonathan stood by David's side, we too can find strength and support through meaningful relationships as we pursue our own purposes and dreams.

The unexpected help will show up. Build with them. Assemble with the people that are just as excited as you are about the journey. You will know them by the fruit they produce. They will always be working ahead of you. They will always think about the work as much as you do.

Build them up.

Why?

They are God sent.

When you are building and implementing structure, whether it's a ministry, media marketplace or running for an office, your assistance is going to come from those that you least expected. Sometimes, the individuals who come alongside us may not fit our preconceived notions or align with our initial expectations. However, they bring unique skills, perspectives, and contributions that prove invaluable to our journey. They may possess talents or resources that complement our own and fill the gaps in our abilities. Oftentimes, we will hang our hope on the help of others and not the hand of God who's working behind the scenes. Never get so caught up in the help that we place all our hope in them. I have experienced both failures and victories. While the failures may have been disheartening, it is important to remember that they are part of the process and starting work is the biggest step you can take. No matter how big or small, maximize where you are.

There is an inner enemy you will have to contend with all the days of your life. You will encounter this enemy. You will need to face and overcome it. It will leave for a season but it will return. Especially when you are starting something new. This inner enemy may manifest itself as self-doubt, insecurities, or critical inner voices that discourage you from pursuing your ministry. It can create obstacles and challenges within your own mind, hindering your progress and preventing you from taking bold steps forward. This adversarial giant will challenge your identity. It will even come from others who mean you well.

Are you ready for it?

The adversary of comparison.

Comparison is an identity thief. Identity theft is the number one crime in the world. The spirit of comparison, while building, is sent to snatch, erase, and obliterate your unique fingerprint off the Earth. There is absolutely nothing wrong with gleaming from others to learn, yet the spirit of comparison will have you taking measurements of yourself compared against others.

Are you anointed enough?

Are you gifted enough like this one or that one?

The spirit of comparison works to erase our individuality and replace it with an imitation or replica of someone else. It convinces us that our worth is determined by external factors such as material possessions, achievements, or appearance, rather than recognizing and embracing our own unique strengths, talents, and the hand of God who's working behind the scenes.

*"For we dare not make ourselves of the number, or compare ourselves with some that commend themselves: but they measuring themselves by themselves, and comparing themselves among themselves, are not wise." (2 Cor 10:12 KJV)*

The world doesn't need another Bishop TD Jakes, he is him already. The world needs you to be you. During my first year, there was a constant battle to build or to be like this one or that one because of their success. If we will be honest, there isn't a person that you don't know of that at some point did not compare themselves. That stage is when you're trying to figure out and learning to trust what you possess. It's not always that we don't trust God. Sometimes, we don't trust ourselves because we failed ourselves countless times. However, there will come a point when you will discover that what you have is greater than you can ever imagine. Here's the newsflash, others can see it sometimes before you can. All you need is divine development. What is divine development? You need "a Jonathan." A Johnathan type mentor who understands what you have and is willing to be a tour guide into the next season. Trust there are some associates around you now, that you haven't acknowledged yet, that know you got it. They can see you have the "it" factor. Please don't make the mistake and think you have arrived just because you had a few victories and wins. It's about maintaining a mindset of continuous learning and self-improvement. There are always new challenges to face. Stay low. Stay humble.

I was figuring things out. I was discovering my personal genius in those stages. The genesis and the genius of you must be guarded with prayer and fasting. These practices can provide clarity, guidance, spiritual strength to navigate challenges, and the ability to make wiser decisions allowing you to seek a deeper connection with God. Discouragement will make you quit and make poor decisions. The mind must be guarded and constantly renewed. I cannot stress this enough! I have counseled great men and women who have quit in the height of success.

*"And be not conformed to this world: but be ye transformed by the renewing of your mind, that ye may prove what is that good, and acceptable, and perfect, will of God." (Romans 12:2 KJV)*

I have known people that have this verse memorized. They can say it forward and backwards with ease yet when the rubber meets the road, they're going to need to have this in their hearts. The transformation is the process but the Will of God is the end result. Our unrenewed thinking will fight against everything: your releasing, proclaiming, and prophesying. Yes, the parts of us we haven't surrendered to God will fight against everything.

Throughout your journey, you will go through stages of self-discovery and personal growth. It was in these very stages myself that I unlocked my true potential and embraced my unique genius. I did not see it at first. I heard what I heard. God said what God said. I just went through the process and trusted the process. It required diligent effort and a commitment to renew my own thinking - to replace negative thoughts and self-doubt with the power of the Word and a belief in my capabilities to do what God put in me to do. It's like I changed the lens through which I saw myself and stepped outside of my comfort zone, surrendering to God's Will with humility and trust.

When challenges arise, which they will, you will be faced with whatever the facts say and whatever your faith is saying. Never underestimate the power of your declarations. The 'inner me' and life, itself, will use unbelief, comparison, and people walking out - to make you doubt the very Word declared over your life. The journey of life will be filled with moments that test our faith, make us doubt the promises, and make us doubt the declarations spoken over our lives. That inner voice of doubt and the challenges we face will try to overshadow the truth of God's Word. He will fight against you relentlessly.

When you look at the facts, will it deplete your faith?

Facts are always trying to beat faith. Nevertheless, faith will beat the facts every time. Faith is telling you to get over the facts.

Faith says, "I don't care what the facts say. Go look again, try again. Just start!".

Again, you don't have time to go back and forth with anything or anyone. God said what He said. Let me help you, the cavalry isn't coming, the rescue team isn't coming. When you start, you've got to trust God. Don't look for a lot of people to understand where you are, as it relates to your starting process. Many will come with great ideas but sometimes the great ideas are not the God ideas. You will be rejected by those that are close and by those you've trusted. Nevertheless, stay the course! You will not be able to go into a store and purchase faith for $9.99 in Walmart. Faith is not for sale but faith from the start is on the inside of you." When I talk about having faith, I am referring to a deep trust and belief in something or someone greater than ourselves, our belief in God. It is our spiritual conviction that goes beyond what we can see or touch. Faith starts as a seed planted within us, that ignites our connection to the divine.

*"For I say, through the grace given unto me, to every man that is among you, not to think of himself more highly than he ought to think; but to think soberly, according as God hath dealt to every man the measure of faith." (Romans 12:3 KJV)*

Looking crazy is a part of the faith Journey. Look at it this way: along the journey there will be many stops to pick up people and to drop them off. I'll never forget one of my mentors who is pastor of a great church said to me, "Son, you must wear people loosely" - meaning that people are going to transition, change, and quit. Don't be emotionally invested to the point that it paralyzes you, when they move on. The responsibility of the vision belongs to you. There will be moments where you are your only supporter, the only investor, the only usher, the only greeter, and the only marketing personnel. That is your season of development. Let me be real clear. Divine development.

"Why is that, Pastor?" you may ask.

You can't train people in areas to do a job in excellence if you have never done it or have *no* idea of how it works. Let me tell you, this greatness is not developed instantaneously. Greatness is developed with a consistency of doing the work. Some people just want to encourage others to follow them and for them to point and direct people on what to do. It's going to be a complete fail. Why? You must put your hand to the work. It will not be overnight. Greatness is not overnight. You cannot just talk about it through mere words of encouragement, you have to be about it in action. It is a product of consistent effort, dedication, and hard work. Simply telling others to follow us and expecting them to achieve greatness without putting in the necessary work, is fictitious, and will inevitably lead to failure.

Now that we've gotten that out the way, stewardship should be your main focus. It should be at the forefront of your lives because it shows that you have an understanding that everything we have is a gift from God and that you are responsible for using your own gifts wisely. It's about you recognizing the value of your time, your talents, your resources, and choosing to utilize these gifts and talents in ways that benefit others and honor God. Get this in your spirit now starting with stewardship. Stewardship of time, finances, people, and possessions is equally as important as the process and the transformation. If you don't care about stewardship, later as you grow, it will show that you didn't care.

Starting is where you must focus heavily when beginning on stewardship. Don't focus your attention on the possessions of clothes, cars and cribs. All that is to make yourself seem relevant or that you have arrived. No! Take this time to invest in the vision God has given to you. Look closely at the deficiencies that God is trying to build in you. Trust me, no one starts with everything. When you begin, God will use people to show you what you need to work on, if you can discern your surroundings.

Look at the people surrounding you and ask yourself:

What am I learning from them?

What do I appreciate about them?

Write this down and you will begin to see what's needed or appreciated and what God has done.

Being in constant frustration is a sign that you need to slow things down and have patience. Sometimes what you tried isn't working. It can be a reminder that sometimes your efforts are not going to yield the desired results. Instead of staying in discouragement, instead of overlooking important details because of frustration, or neglecting to give things its proper time to unfold naturally, recognize that this can be an opportunity for growth and learning. God could be slowing you down to reveal to you a critical piece you're missing.

Don't despise the genesis of what you're launching. It is so easy to get into a hurry to see the finished product that you leave out important ingredients. My grandmother, who helped raise me, would bake cakes from time to time. She understood what it took to make the cake. She didn't have to look at the ingredients on the box to make it. She would make cakes from scratch. I remember once she put a cake in the oven and would not allow me to run through the house. She would yell to me, "Boy, stop running in and out *my* house before you make my cake fall".

I didn't understand what she meant, until later, that the ingredients that were in the cake had to have a controlled environment. An atmosphere where there wasn't a bunch of movement, shaking, twisting and turns. The temperature will make the cake rise but the suddening movements end up making it fall. I hope you caught that. What was supposed to rise will end up falling if there's too much movement, twisting, turning and shaking in the atmosphere. If you are doing the most and are unsettled, always trying to do what you are not called to do or what you are not good at doing, this will cause you as a person not to rise up in the areas where you should be rising or becoming great in.

I could smell that cake that she baked throughout the house. I would go outside and smell the cake through the screen door. One of the things that I learned from her was that when she would take that cake out of the oven, but before she would give me a piece, she would: take a toothpick, stick the toothpick inside the cake, pull it back out, and examine the toothpick. I would be ready for a piece. The toothpick was the indicator to her whether or not the cake was ready. If the ingredients came back up on the toothpick when she pulled it out, that meant that the cake wasn't ready. Let me say that again. It can rise but still not be ready because the ingredients have not fully come together.

I really want those of you that are reading this to grasp that you can have a quick rise but that doesn't mean you're ready. The key to the cake being ready is when the toothpick goes in and none of the ingredients come out. You may look crazy but start.

While you are on your way to the next chapter (and I don't mean only the next chapter of the book but the next chapter of your life), expect attacks. Expect to overcome it. Expect lies of the enemy to flood your thoughts. Expect a level of insecurity to question whether or not you got the goods for the assignment. The warfare will intensify when you are about to launch anything major especially when God is in it. The desire to remain in the same place will be on the menu with a side order of familiarity and comfort. Whatever you do, start. Do what God says even if you're nervous, full of anxiety. Do it with gritted teeth forging forward.

*C. H.  Spurgeon "our anxiety does not empty tomorrow of its sorrows, but only empties today of its strengths.*

CHAPTER 6

**I Look Crazy but Character is Key**

After our first location in the basement of a video store we moved at least three more times. One of the many lessons I learned at my second and third locations was how to handle deception and the leaders who had these bad business practices. I learned not to compromise your integrity because you want to accomplish a task. I don't know what it was but we had a propensity to always find ourselves behind something. We always seem to pick locations where the church is hidden in the area. The first location was behind an old video store in the basement. Let me explain, the video store was on the main street but behind and under that building was where my church was located.

The second location we will just call it, Rainbow. There was nothing magical or lucky about it but it was indeed colorful on the inside. It wasn't a result of mere chance or coincidence, but rather a deliberate display of color and symbolism. The lion motif adorned every corner, exuding strength and majesty. The seats were a regal purple, contrasting beautifully against the deep blue carpet that stretched across the floor. Flags adorned the walls, representing the diverse backgrounds and cultures of the congregation. Even the walls themselves bloomed with delicate floral patterns, there were pictures on every wall, while fresh flowers graced the floor, adding a touch of beauty and life to the space. Everywhere you looked, there was a rich tapestry of decor, creating an environment that stimulated the senses and invited all who entered to experience the depth and beauty of worship in a truly immersive way. Like I said earlier, nothing magical or lucky about it but it was indeed colorful on the inside.

The Rainbow location was next to a transmission shop that had broken down cars all around it. Oftentimes, people would pull up at our services thinking that the place was packed. However, it wasn't. It was just the broken down cars that were parked over in the parking lot, next to our cars. My wife and I would often laugh as we would pull up at the place. We'd say, "It's packed today!", knowing full well, we knew it wasn't.

This location was also the place where God was sending new sons and daughters that loved the ministry. This location was also the catalyst to the discovery of our DNA for ministry. I clearly understood that our ministry was unique and that I wasn't called to the 'bright and shiny people' at the time. There's nothing wrong with them, but God had not sent them *into* my assignment, yet. The Rainbow location helped me to see the potential in people that didn't look like much to the natural eye but they were powerful men and women of God. Prayer was the focus.

I am sure, without a shadow of a doubt, that God was teaching me more about character. The owners of the building wanted to hide the money we were paying for rent. Originally they had agreed to give us a W-9 but later changed their mind. Many issues will show up and challenges will arise that will hinder your development if character has been compromised. You don't want to look like a Mercedes Benz S500 2023 on the outside but have a Yugo engine on the inside. It's undesirable to have a flashy exterior while lacking substance on the inside. Just imagine what that would look like, encountering a car that looks like the luxurious Mercedes Benz S500 of 2023. Its exterior exudes elegance and prestige, but upon closer inspection, you discover it has a Yugo engine—a symbol of poor performance and unreliability. I am telling you this extends to life itself. Consider both the external appearances and internal qualities.

While people are out here projecting a successful and attractive image to the world I must raise the attention that they must also just as equally cultivate depth and substance within themselves. It is crucial for the ministry. We must strive for authenticity and ensure that our internal parts and motivation match the outward presentation showing that God's hand is on us.

Some leaders fall in love with the idea of looking successful but aren't producing anything. Character issues hinder productivity; it reminds me of Jesus and the fig tree. It looks like it's ready from a distance but the closer you get, you discover that it's missing something.   Fruit!!

*"And on the morrow, when they were come from Bethany, he was hungry: And seeing a fig tree afar off having leaves, he came, if haply he might find anything thereon: and when he came to it, he found nothing but leaves; for the time of figs was not yet. And Jesus answered and said unto it, No man eat fruit of thee hereafter for ever. And his disciples heard it." (Mark 11:12-14 KJV)*

Jesus was hungry and when seeing the fig tree full of leaves, He expected to find fruit there. It appeared from a distance very fruitful. However, when He got there, it had no fruit. You will notice a conversation, it says that Jesus answered the fig tree. This is quite interesting because it's suggesting that the fig tree *said* something to Jesus.

He answered that tree, telling it: "No man would eat from it ever again".

Jesus answered to the very thing that was unproductive and deceptive. Jesus requires we produce. Fruit is what speaks louder than the words you could ever express.

When I say, " Jesus requires we produce", it means that Jesus expects us to bear fruit in our lives. This goes beyond mere words or outward appearances; it refers to being productive and impactful in our actions and behaviors. Producing fruit implies making a positive difference in the lives of others, exhibiting moral behavior, and embodying the teachings and character of Christ. It's a call to be fruitful in our faith, displaying love, kindness, compassion, and other virtues that have a tangible and transformative effect on those around us.

The idea that "fruit speaks louder than words" emphasizes that our actions and the impact we have on others carry greater weight than mere verbal expressions. It highlights the importance of living out our faith and demonstrating its power through the positive influence we have on others. True fruitfulness lies not in empty promises or superficial displays, but in the tangible results of a life lived in alignment with Christ's teachings.

*"Ye have not chosen me, but I have chosen you, and ordained you, that ye should go and bring forth fruit, and that your fruit should remain: that whatsoever ye shall ask of the Father in my name, he may give it to you." (John 15:16 KJV)*

Character is the life sustaining source for anything you're going to build. Character tells others you care. If people believe you are shady or have damaged clients then family and friends will stay away from you like the Ebola plague. There was an issue that I ran into the second location. I was eager to leave the basement of the video store, the first location, because there wasn't enough room. I found this second location and happily paid the first month's rent and deposit. I just wanted my people in a better position to do a greater work for God. I counted up the cost and made the move. The owner of the facility agreed for a certain amount to be paid every month, not once, did we ever miss a payment. We were there for six to eight months.

At the end of the year, we asked the owner, who was an apostle in the Lord's Church, to send us the W-9, so we could manage our books. Well, that woman of God refused. She refused to do any such thing yet still wanted to keep the income she was making a secret from the IRS. This shows something, her ministry was struggling and basically non-existent. This breach in her character explained why her ministry was suffering.

I immediately got on the phone with her asking, "What is the issue with filling out the W-9, which is the correct thing to do?"

With a very sharp tone, she *told me*, "I am *not* going to do it because I *don't* want to".

"This was *not* the agreement", I contested.

"Well", she snapped back, "You *are* using the space and there is *no* issue there".

At that point I decided to leave that conversation alone because I knew it was going left fast and both her attitude plus her actions were wrong. No matter what I said, it would end with her same response.

Now, because she did not fill out the W-9 for us, it appears as if I pocketed the money, based on the available financial records. Nevertheless, I didn't pocket a dime. So there I was stuck. Stuck in a position where I couldn't find a new location to get out from under this unethical business practice. Long story short, I got in tax trouble because of it. Now here's the test: would I be transparent with the people I'm pastoring? or hide it?

Without a question, I shared this information with the team about the dilemma we were having. First, I had to take a hit from the IRS because of the apostles' action. Secondly, we had to find, yet again, another location to worship. Never be afraid to disclose to your team matters that challenge your process. They are helping you build. You will be surprised how understanding and supportive they will be. Hiding issues that need to be disclosed will eventually damage the trust you've built and trust is paramount.

Satan will try to disturb your assignment with God. He will get you in your feelings in order for you to make an impulsive and unwise decision. As much as I didn't like looking indecisive and unstable, I had to move yet again. I was constantly battling what the people thought and what others on the outside said.

"Jesus, he's moving again".

"Something must be wrong over there at Bethlehem City".

All of this stuff was weighing heavy on my mind. I soon discovered the main enemy of focus and vision was fear. Fear that you will fail. Fear it won't work. It can be difficult for us to do the things of God because we're so accustomed to the natural realm. Seeing only from the natural realm when drama hits.

In the natural realm, there is a power I can see that is a kind of faith and vision operating at the human level. That human level will have you balking when you should be moving. The spiritual realm is the power I can't see. It is trusting a God I can't see. It is to believe that even though something looks bad it will work out for my good.

After getting past my feelings about transitioning so quickly from one location to the next, we ended up at another place that checked all the boxes. It had the amount of seating that we needed. It passed the eyeball test and finally, the property was on the main road. We will call this place, Freeman.

Freeman was a place that truly challenged my faith; it was more in rent than I previously had to spend. It was as if God was using this place to stretch me in faith. This phase of ministry was yet another learning experience that I would soon encounter. This was a place where my faith was stretched but it was also the place where we grew in numbers. We experienced tremendous growth. We had visitors every Sunday. We were growing in numbers but not in financial support.

Oftentimes, we equate a lot of people to enormous financial support. Trust me, that wasn't the case in my journey. I became frustrated right before I left the Rainbow location. I remember we stayed in a small house that we rented in order to save money. My wife and I called it, "The Shack". One Saturday morning, we went downstairs into the garage that we made into a small office. This is the place that I would often go to pray at home. I got my face on and began to pray. I asked God to help us because we were struggling so badly financially. I was using my money. The money from my job is what I used to pay just about for everything. This was to be expected when you believe in the vision God has given you. Yet, I remember when I began to complain to God about the challenges I was having.

I said, "God, I need some lawyers, doctors, business owners, and some people that could fund this vision".

The Lord responded back to me and he said these words: "Jameson, I am sending you the misfits".

When he said that, I immediately shifted out of crying into astonishment.

"What?" I exclaimed. "The misfits?"

I promise you, I am not making this stuff up.

I then heard the Lord laugh. "Oooooh Jameson, did we soon forget that you were once a misfit".

My mind went back to my former life. I immediately saw myself in my past, in my present and also in my future. I begin to weep passionately. I was once a misfit, once a part of misfits and I was reminded of how God brought me out of all of it.

God said, "Yes! I will send the misfits and they shall work wonders among you".

This is what God said to me that these people, the misfits, were coming to work and the wonders meant they would do things that would amaze you. I had a drug addict stop buying drugs and help send me to a leadership conference because he heard my desire. He led by example. He took action and donated financially to ensure I would be in attendance.

Pure coincidence? No. No. No. This was Wonder!

God reminded me of my past as a misfit, someone who didn't fit into societal norms or expectations. The flood of memories brought forth a deep sense of gratitude as I reflected on the 'wonders' of my own journey. God spoke words of reassurance and purpose to me. God changed my view of the people he was sending. He renewed my thinking to see them how he sees them. His words reverberated through the depths of my being. I found myself immersed in the resounding proclamation of God that echoed in my ears, "Yes! I will send the misfits, and they shall work wonders among you."

Things started to happen supernaturally.

A woman who was riding by our church, stopped in for a visit. My wife had conversations with her after the service. During their conversational exchange, I noticed my wife waving at me to come to her. What happened next blew my mind.

The woman said these words: "I was riding by your church and the Lord told me to turn around and to come in and give you $500".

This kind of stuff was happening.

Pure coincidence? No. No. No. This was Wonder!

There were many wonders. But, I have a favorite supernatural experience to share. This particular supernatural move blessed my life. I was talking about one Sunday service that stood out. I had made mention that I would love to go to the TD Jakes leadership conference. I wanted to become a better leader for the people God called me to pastor. Now what's about to happen next may shock you.

There was a gentleman coming to my church that was a drug addict. After hearing me say "I would love to go to TD Jakes leadership conference", at the end of the service, he expressed wanting to say something to the whole congregation. I had no idea what he was about to say.

He grabbed a mic, told me to come closer to him and said, "Pastor, I want to say something to you. We are going to send you to the leadership conference".

Honestly me hearing that, I'm thinking he's just talking. He reaches into his pocket and pulls out two hundred dollars to give me in order that I may go to the conference. Not only that, he started a campaign with a few of the members in the church to raise enough money to pay for my flight and hotel to send me to the leadership conference. This man put down crack cocaine just to send me to a conference so that I may learn from other leaders. It reminded me of what the Lord said, "They shall work wonders among you".

You heard me right, a drug addict stopped doing drugs just to send me to my first leadership conference. While other groups of attendees were at the conference from corporations, churchs, and businesses, I was there off of the obedience of a crack addict God used. While other groups of attendees at the conference represented corporations, churches, and businesses, I found myself there through the obedience of a crack addict whom God used. This was a truly remarkable and unexpected experience for me. I have never heard of this in my life.

What a powerful and unexpected encounter! A person struggling with addiction and misfortune became an instrument through which God worked to exhibit selflessness and provide the means for me, the pastor, to participate in a leadership conference that others attended from reputable organizations and establishments. In this unexpected turn of events, this incident exemplifies the fulfillment of that divine declaration by God, "they shall work wonders among you." That conference catapulted my confidence as the leader of the church.

Here is what I wanted you to understand: some of the greatest support will come from the least likely people you would have never thought God would use. Let me share that a prostitute named Rahab, the least likely one, was used as a hero to save the Israelite spies who were doing military recon. Rahab not only hid the spies from the authorities but also provided them with vital information and ensured their safe escape. Through Rahab, God preserved the lives of the spies who also played a crucial role in the conquest of Jericho and the fulfillment of His divine plan. God's ways are higher than our own, and He has the power to work through individuals who may be seen as outcasts or misfits. God's grace is available to all. He can use anyone who is willing to step out in faith and obedience. God will work through anyone!

*I know that the LORD has given you this land and that a great fear of you has fallen on us, so that all who live in this country are melting in fear because of you. We have heard how the LORD dried up the water of the Red Sea for you when you came out of Egypt, and what you did to Sihon and Og, the two kings of the Amorites east of Jordan, whom you completely destroyed. When we heard of it, our hearts melted in fear and everyone's courage failed because of you, for the LORD your God is God in heaven above and on the earth below. "Now then, please swear to me by the LORD that you will show kindness to my family, because I have shown kindness to you. Give me a sure sign that you will spare the lives of my father and mother, my brothers and sisters, and all who belong to them— and that you will save us from death." (Joshua 2:9-13 NIV)*

These supernatural moves became a part of our church culture. We were growing in numbers and partners were maturing. Understand and know that as you begin to experience growth and maturity the enemy of division will plant seeds to hinder this process. It's important to know that sometimes the attack slips in because of our own oversight, our own lack of focus.

There was a prophet I brought into my church because I believed that he would be a blessing to my people. He came to share the Word of the Lord, which was good and timely. However, it was *after* he left that we had a major problem. To my utter disbelief, I learned that he had been privately reaching out to the members of my church, seeking to lure them away to his own ministry. The hurt and betrayal I felt were unimaginable. I was shocked! He began to reach out to the people in *my* church to pull them into *his* ministry. I had warmly welcomed this prophet and eagerly anticipated the blessings he would bring, yet what he brought was this revelation that shattered my heart. I had believed that our relationship was built on mutual respect and a shared commitment to serving God's people. It was devastating to realize that appearances can be deceiving, and even those we trust can have hidden motives. This attack slipped in because of my own oversight.

I discovered this through the brave confession of one of my daughters in church. She shared with me the extent of what she knew about the prophet's actions. She revealed that he had been undermining the ministry, discrediting me, and attempting to turn the congregation against me through private messages.

I even saw Facebook Live streams that were done covertly with subliminal messages to speak about me. I had an idea that he was doing this. Yet, I had to see for myself and went back to watch the replays. I was hurt but I understood who was in operation.

God gave me an understanding of my role in caring for the church community and the tending of His flock. There may be spiritually mature individuals within the church but the collective body of believers is still relatively young and inexperienced, just like a two-year-old child. This means that the church is still developing, growing, and learning in its faith journey. I made the mistake of bringing in an unknown voice instead of a trusted voice to edify my people to another level of maturity.

It is important for new church Pastors to take close care of their 'baby' church that's just been born. The church may require gentle teaching, guidance, and support to help it mature and thrive in its spiritual journey. Also an understanding that every babysitter (any voice outside of your house) does not have the same heart as the parents nor the same love for the children that they're raising. So, it is important to make sure that every voice that comes into your house is vetted and researched.

When building something we must always make sure that the voices close to our ears are well discerned. What do I mean? We must carefully evaluate and discern the advice and influence of those who are in close proximity to us. We must take the time to know them extremely well. Often, our zeal for getting better overrides our wisdom for seeing well. Our eagerness for improvement should not overshadow our ability. Businesses, athletes, and relationships have fallen because what looked good to them really wasn't good for them. Blindly following others for what may appear good on the surface can lead to negative consequences in various areas of life. I am a prophet and a leader who only follows God.

I immediately called my church together and explained to them that this was inappropriate and asinine for any leader to do this behind any pastor's back. Ninety-eight of my people took heed, two percent continued on to follow and support him, until their eyes became opened. They have since apologized and changed directions.

When things like this happen it is your duty as the leader to address it. Address these issues even if you look like the bad guy. As we progressed forward, things were going well for the ministry. There was no special marketing strategy I was using. I just obeyed the voice of God and he used every hopeless circumstance for my good.

There was yet another bump on the road that would shake the church. There was a deep curve that I was going around, a little too fast, that had the potential to cause me to go off the cliff, crashing at the bottom with a big explosion. Trouble was coming! I was being watched by the owner of the building. One Sunday after church he pulled me to the side to have a conversation.

"I have been watching you", "He said, "I've seen the miracles of God and the growth of the ministry. What are you doing?"

"Honestly I don't know", I replied, "I am just obeying God, man."

He went on to say, "I need you to speak to some other pastors. I've been pastoring for twenty years and I have never seen someone grow so quickly".

"Thank you. I can't do it because I don't feel ready. I am still learning and growing."

"Well", he said, "In a few months, I am going to raise your rent because it's time. You have been here for a year."

I said, "Yes sir", and the conversation ended.

I noticed that he went from helping us start up the service with the equipment to sitting in the services and attending. I didn't have an issue with it because we had no problems so far. A few months passed and the air conditioner went out. He said he would fix it but it never got fixed. I called him. He just went on and explained that the other tenants were behind on their rent. I complained constantly every week and the air conditioning still didn't get repaired. I was concerned about the people coming to my church being in the heat.

When I called yet again. He shared with me the cost to get the AC repaired, which wasn't my issue, but because of the people I pastor, I helped and paid the rent in advance. It was repaired for a moment and then it went out again. He moved us to a smaller suite in the same building during a mid-week service because of the problem with the AC. Keep in mind, I am paying the same price on rent, on time.

On that Sunday morning, as our church gathered for worship, I couldn't help but notice that the air conditioning would intermittently work and then suddenly cut out. It became evident to me that there was an underlying issue causing this disruption: the owner of the building where our church was located was facing financial difficulties. He kept cutting the AC off midway through our services and also relocated us to a smaller place for bible study. He did this to cut his utility cost. This revelation struck a chord of concern within me because it meant that our church's stability and future were now in jeopardy.

The owner called for a meeting. I took the opportunity to express my concerns. I candidly explained to the owner that the square footage we were paying for was not being made available to us as initially promised. I hoped to find a resolution that would restore our church's stability and ensure that we could continue fulfilling our mission effectively. It was important for me to advocate for the rights and needs of our church community, seeking a fair and equitable arrangement that honored our financial commitment and allowed us to utilize the space as agreed upon.

I knew it was my responsibility to hold integrity as the Pastor in this challenging circumstance. My primary responsibility was to protect and advocate for the well-being of our congregation, both spiritually and practically. I aimed to find a mutually beneficial solution without unnecessary hindrances. But this issue did not get resolved. I was still paying the same price.

Towards the end of the meeting the owner introduces me to his wife and says, "Going forward she will handle all of the business for the property."

Then he asked me to do something strange. He insisted that instead of making the rent check payable to the church, as per our agreement and lease terms, I should make it payable to a new company they were starting. Realizing that this request went against our agreed-upon terms, I politely explained to the owner that I couldn't comply with his request. I reminded him of our initial agreement and emphasized that it was not stated in the lease agreement. Despite his insistence, I remained firm in my position, expressing that I could not deviate from the agreed-upon terms. He asked me to consider it and again I assured him that I could not do that.

First of the month rolls around and rent is due between the first and the fifth of every month. I received an unexpected call on the third day of the month. The owner placed pressure on me to pay the rent before the designated deadline.

I told him, "No problem".

He told me to speak to his wife when I'm on my way with the check.

I wrote the check payable to the church that owns the property as the agreement stated, in adherence to the original agreement.

The wife proceeds to call me and ask me what time I was coming by the property to give her the check. I told her the time I would arrive. To my surprise, she insisted that the check must be made payable to the company she and her husband had established. Once again, I calmly reiterated that this was not what we had agreed upon, referring to the lease agreement. This disagreement led to her becoming upset and threatening to involve her husband.

"I'm going to call my husband," she said to me, "because I don't like what you're saying to me."

I found her reaction puzzling, that I said, "What am I saying that is so awful that you feel offended."

My refusal to comply with her request was based on the agreement we had discussed in the office.

She replied, "You're not willing to do what I asked you to do."

"Ma'am, call your husband," I said, "because I told your husband and you in the office that I was not going to do that and he asked me to consider it. I have already considered that I wasn't going to do it."

Please keep in mind, it was important for me to remain steadfast in upholding the terms of the lease agreement and protecting the best interests of our church. Having experienced challenges with that former property, which had already burned me (remember Rainbow?) taught me the importance of adhering to agreed-upon terms and not succumbing to undue pressure.

Here I am having been a faithful tenant, never late, and paid rent several times early to help him. Now there is pressure to pay rent which I've never had from them. It gave me a great pause. The sudden change in their behavior and the pressure raised concerns. I had to pause to reconsider the dynamics of our landlord-tenant relationship and their approach left me feeling apprehensive. I couldn't help but draw comparisons to the past negative experiences of the other locations we had. It became clear that I needed to navigate this situation with caution and carefully evaluate the motivations and intentions of the property owners.

My phone rang. I picked it up. I knew who it was, the husband. As soon as I say hello..

In a rage, he began to yell, "I don't appreciate how you handled my wife."

I said, "I've done nothing to your wife other than stand firm on what I told you in your office. She did not like the fact that I would not do what she asked me to do. I have the check in hand. I headed to your place but it's not written out to your company. It is written out to what we agreed upon in the lease agreement."

"You know what," He said, "I still don't like it and I think the next month should be your last month in my facility."

At that moment when he said that I said, "Sir next month will not be my last month. Today is my last day and I won't need your building anymore."

We ended that call and I thought to myself, *What have I done?* I knew what I was doing was right yet, here I am again needing another place to go. Here we are again with events leading up to a moment that becomes challenging and unexpected.

On that Wednesday, I felt the weight of uncertainty pressing upon me. I've got to tell my people in just a few hours we have no place to worship. As I sat in my car, for about 3 minutes, the gravity of the situation weighed heavily on my heart and mind. I was confused, angry, and hurt.

How would I break the news to my congregation?

How would they react to the sudden news that we had no place to gather and worship?

I closed my eyes, seeking guidance in prayer, desperately asking God to intervene and provide a way forward. In the midst of my silent plea, all of a sudden my phone rings, disrupting the heavy atmosphere in the car. With a mix of surprise and curiosity, I picked up the call. It was a pastor friend of mine who called me out of the blue, with no knowledge of the challenges I was currently facing. Not even my wife knew what happened. It had only been approximately 3 to 5 minutes. It was as if God had heard my prayers and sent this person to offer a glimmer of hope in my challenging hour.

Pastor John says to me, "You were in my spirit and I felt that something was wrong and you needed to talk to me right away."

I explained to him what happened and how I had no place to go.

"That's the reason why I called," He said, "Don't you worry 'bout a thing. You can have your worship services in my church. Also, don't worry about paying me for the next two months."

Man, oh man! Was I relieved! We had a place to go and worship. Little did I know that moment would mark the beginning of a new chapter, one filled with unexpected blessings, strengthened bonds, and a deepened reliance on God's unfailing guidance. The events of that Wednesday became a powerful testimony. However I've got to tell my church again that we've got to move. With honesty and transparency I took a deep breath and began to share the circumstances that had unfolded and the difficult decision I had made. I shared with them everything that happened. They were supportive and honored my decision.

A great weight was lifted off of my shoulders. I must tell you. Even though the weight was lifted and I was relieved the next three months, I lost the momentum that we were once carrying. It was a time of adjustment and transition, where the reality of the situation weighed heavily. I lost a great deal of members to the church because of this move. However as I look over it now, I see it in the way God handled Gideon. Gideon, a mighty warrior, started with a sizable army of 30,000 men. However, God had a different plan in mind. He instructed Gideon to reduce his forces, ultimately whittling them down to a mere 300 men to face a formidable enemy. Yes, when God finished handling Gideon, he only had 300 men to go up against an enemy mightier, stronger, and with more soldiers than he could count.

This was the same thing God was doing in my transition, stripping me down to a number that he could use. Though the loss of members and the decline in momentum were painful, I began to recognize that this process was part of God's greater plan for our church. He was stripping me down to a number that only God could get the credit for. We stayed at Pastor John's Church for approximately three to four months.

During our time at Pastor John's Church, I received a divine message from the Lord in March. He told me that within 45 days we would have our own place. This was major for us because every place we've been to was a shared space except for the place called Rainbow. True to His word, within 45 days, God provided us with a permanent home for the next three years. It was an incredible blessing and a testament to His faithfulness. Once again, God was using unexpected circumstances and unlikely sources to demonstrate His power and fulfill His promises. God again was up to something and he was going to show us the Misfits once again.

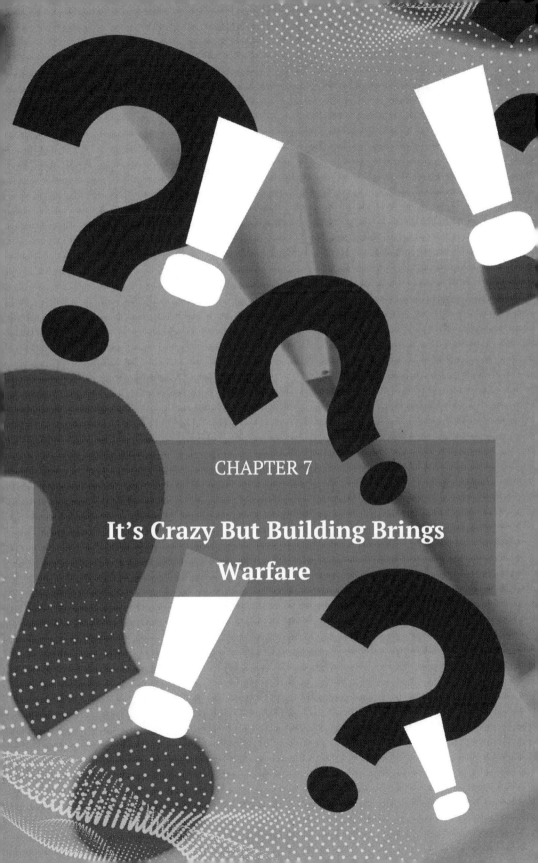

CHAPTER 7

# It's Crazy But Building Brings Warfare

Whenever you begin to launch out, there will always be Warfare. It comes with the territory. Victory comes when we advance through the Warfare. I urge you to press forward through the Warfare, refusing to be deterred by the obstacles you encounter. Nehemiah was a prime example of the Warfare you'll face when you're building something for God. Nehemiah, before he started doing anything, he surveyed the land that he was going to start building on. He remained focused on the mission and the greater purpose, never discussing the intimate details with anybody except God.

*"So I came to Jerusalem, and was there for three days. And I arose in the night, I and some few men with me; neither told any man what my God had put in my heart to do at Jerusalem: neither was there any beast with me, save the beast that I rode upon."*
*(Nehemiah 2:11-12 KJV)*

I believe Nehemiah had an understanding that everyone can't handle the vision God gives and everyone is not going to be on board with the vision you have, even if it benefits them. When you believe with all of your heart that this vision is for you, you must go at it with all you have. That belief in one's vision is essential for pursuing it with unwavering determination.

There's a story about Napoleon Bonaparte and his resolute belief in his vision. He was a French military leader and Emperor who conquered much of Europe in the 19th century. This man was short in stature but big on his vision. He rose to power rapidly because of his heart. Hear me. I'm not saying that he was right. I'm simply saying, when you believe something with all of your heart nothing can knock you off course. Napoleon believed in his vision so much that when he crossed over to a city to conquer it, he would burn the bridge behind him so that the soldiers and everyone with him knew it was either win or die trying.

Again, while I am not suggesting that his decisions were morally right, what can be noted was his level of commitment, determination, and the willingness to take bold risks in his own vision. Imagine how much bolder you must be willing to be and also, how much more committed and determined you must be willing to be to step up into what God's vision is for you. I believed in my vision with all my heart, nothing would knock me off course. "...either win or die trying..."

This message that Napoleon had sent to the enemy impressed upon them that he was going to win or die trying too. The way he saw it, it was either death or victory, win or lose, wounded, beat up, or whatever - "you're going to have to deal with me." That was his thought process. Napoleon conquered much out of his own ambition.

How much more can we who have the backing of God?

Just a few of us Misfits. Here we go, entering a new season and transitioning to a new location.

Winning was the only thing that was on our minds. Why? Because we had lost enough! The taste of losing was unbearable.

God was using losers for champions. So we set out to conquer any challenge we would face.

I was grateful to God we found our newest location. Everything that we needed to start and go forward was supernaturally provided. Even Pastor John showed up to help us to get things together. He was a tremendous help and blessing to the ministry. Friends came and stayed all night to paint, along with the women of Bethlehem City who are resourceful, beautiful, and powerful. These women of my church are amazing. Scratch that, amazing isn't an adequate word to describe them. Those women of God orchestrated the logistics of every equipment and assembled them with precision. They put the chairs together because the men were busy at their jobs. They cleaned, patched holes, and did things that were just mind blowing. I will never forget them. I called them the Women of Wakanda. At every turn, they were found working, serving, pushing, building, and doing whatever they could do to make sure that the plans were executed with excellence.

The vision of the church came together. I could never ascribe to women not being preachers, pastors, leaders, or whatever. One of the strongest moves God made came through the women at my church when we needed help the most. Yes, the men of God were instrumental but even they know, those women of *our* church came through. It's a running joke at my church that when things need to get implemented, call the Women of Wakanda.

God has put people in places that I never expected to help us. Thus the work had begun. It was a great time for our church. But with every transaction there is testing that's coming. The season was on its way to introduce a new warfare, produce divine growth and maturity that the church desperately needed. You heard right, we desperately needed warfare to get us ready for our next level. The Lord showed me this in the Book of Judges.

*"Now these are the nations which the Lord left, to prove Israel by them, even as many of Israel as had not known all the wars of Canaan; only that the generations of the children of Israel might know, to teach them war, at the least such as before knew nothing thereof." (Judges 3:1-2 KJV)*

Here's what's so interesting about that scripture is that *"the Lord left"* the enemies. Oftentimes, we think that the enemies that we are facing are sent by the Devil. In this case they weren't sent by the adversary; they were sent by the advocate which is God. Remember the Holy Spirit led Jesus into the wilderness to be tested.

Adversity and warfare will grow you up. I had to experience my son while I was pastoring, go through depression and rejection. It broke our hearts that we couldn't do anything but pray. We had to walk this thing out with him and the demands of the ministry didn't ask me if I needed a break. The adversity that we began to face made me want to quit several times. There were times when the people I loved, sowed into, and trusted, betrayed me, and left. There was a young lady in our church who purposely was trying to sway people against me; she had a Spirit of Jezebel. This was at the beginning of our newest location. The adversity doesn't ask you if you are ready nor does it wait until you get settled before the attacks begin to bombard your life.

Sunday morning came. The praise and worship went on. This young lady would be totally into the service. However, the moment I would get up to the podium to say anything to share a Word, her head would go down and stay down to show me she was not acknowledging me nor respecting what I was saying. I laughed inside; I knew it was the enemy.

In the beginning when this all started I was puzzled but prayer will always reveal the hearts of people around you. Nevertheless, I never approached her because I knew an evil spirit was in operation. It was such a negative spirit, beyond mere human behavior - harmful, deceitful, manipulative, and contrary to the teachings of God. Please always keep in mind, we are not warring against flesh and blood but spirits. I go through prayer, seek God's wisdom, and rely on His strength to navigate situations to overcome the spiritual battles we face.

God knew that we needed adversity. God knew that we needed to learn the art of war to be prepared for what we were going to have to encounter the next three years. Don't get me wrong, those three years were filled with prophetic moments and prophecies, miracle signs and wonders that would come to pass changing people's lives forever. We saw marriages restored. People delivered from drugs.

One miracle that blessed my life and blessed our ministry was a woman delivered from lesbianism. When I saw this young lady come to the church a few times, I began to have a conversation with the Lord.

"How can I win her to you, Lord?" I discovered that she was a barber.

The Lord said, "Let her cut your hair".

"Oh no, I love my barber I have now and I don't want *no* woman cutting my head."

Then the Lord said, "You're not going to win her. If you want to win her over, let her cut your hair."

I decided to let her cut my hair a few times. She was nice with it. It was one of nicest haircuts I ever had. I couldn't wrap my mind around how neat my line was and my beard was. My judgmental mind was turning flips because God was teaching me something about a struggle I knew little about. I knew she was gifted. Before you know it a few more visits to the lady barber and she joined my church. I won her to the Lord.

She said to me, "Prophet, you spoke to deep dark places in my life that no one knew about except me and God."

She went on to say that while she was in my church she knew the Lord was speaking directly to her through me. She also shared with me that the love my wife and I poured into her, won her over, and changed her mind about God. Our ministry impacted this young lady and spoke to deep and hidden areas of her life, which no one else knew about except herself and God. The transformative power of love my wife and I demonstrated to her had a profound effect, changing her perspective on God. I would later find out it was a rescue mission not an introduction to Jesus. She was once in ministry and knew of Jesus. Life challenges had shaken her faith, leading her to doubt His presence and goodness. God used my wife and I to rescue her from a dark place.

When we engage in a rescue mission, our aim is to bring deliverance, healing, and restoration to individuals who are in desperate need of God's intervention. It's not just about introducing them to Jesus. To accomplish this, it requires a higher level, it means going beyond surface-level interactions, it involves walking alongside them through their struggles, providing a listening ear, offering guidance, counsel, and extending a helping hand. Rescue missions require a more comprehensive approach that addresses the root causes. It's important to understand that it's not a quick or easy process and we must be willing to journey with individuals through it and support them along the way. By engaging in a rescue mission, we demonstrate God's love in action. We become vessels through which His power and grace can flow, bringing hope and restoration. It's a call to embody the hands and feet of Jesus, extending His healing touch and walking with others on their journey towards wholeness. We don't know the life journey of people but God does. We had lost touch with her for a few months when transitioning from Freeman location to Pastor John.

After we moved to our new location, we encountered a challenge when my musicians quit, leaving us with no one to play during our Sunday morning worship. To address this, we would often contract musicians to play the keyboard. This arrangement continued for several months. However, on one specific Sunday, the musician we hired turned out to be exceptionally untalented. The music during our worship service was far from beautiful, and it posed a significant challenge for us. To add to the situation, on that same day, we had planned a fellowship dinner after church to foster closer relationships among our members. During this gathering, a deacon and I found ourselves engaged in a conversation discussing the issue with the performance — both in terms of the musical aspect of worship and the fellowship experience.

As we stood in the doorway of the church the young lady who God delivered from lesbianism overheard our conversation about the musician. Keep in mind that she has been with us for a few months. God was saving a Misfit for this moment. She heard my complaint about how awful the musician was and how we needed to do something. We needed to find someone that was consistent and that could play with excellence. She walked over to me and she said to me, "Pastor, I can play the keyboard."

With a smirk on my face, I said to her jokingly but skeptical, "You can't play no keyboard".

"Yes I can!" She replied.

Honestly I was very apprehensive but I said to her anyway, "Well, walk over there and let me see."

As she started playing, an incredible sound filled the room, leaving me in awe. The music that flowed from the keyboard was not only melodious but also carried a prophetic essence that resonated deeply within my spirit and created a sense of wonder and amazement.

At that moment, the deacon and I exchanged astonished glances, realizing that this talented musician had been among us all along, yet we had somehow missed her gift. What a powerful reminder that sometimes the solution to our problems can be right in our midst, waiting to be discovered. I want you to know there is someone right now in your presence that is designed to solve a problem you're encountering. Do not overlook anyone. Once again, God reminded me that "the misfits will work wonders among you". I won't share her testimony but to this day this powerful woman of God is still with us as a part of our church community as we all celebrate the power of God's work in each of our lives.

Indeed, we should never discount anyone, for we do not know how God will work through them to help us move forward into the next season. The story of Nehemiah serves as a powerful reminder of this truth. He was a servant of God, faced with the daunting task of rebuilding the walls of Jerusalem. In his endeavor, Nehemiah used everybody in the city. He rallied the people and united them under a common cause. He recognized that each person had a role to play and that their collective efforts were crucial to the success of the mission. Never discount any one. It is important to remember that God can use anyone, regardless of their background or status, to contribute to our journey. We should not underestimate the potential impact of those around us.

When Nehemiah asked, "Is there not a cause?" He was highlighting the significance of their shared purpose and calling. Likewise, we should always be mindful of the causes that God has placed in our hearts and be open to collaborating with others who share a similar vision. Their presence in our lives may have been ordained to help us fulfill our purpose and reach the next season.

God allows adverse situations as a catalyst for growth to bring us to a spiritual maturity as it reveals both the true nature of others and ourselves; it brings out the worst in some and best in others. Think about it, adversity has helped you see the enemy you didn't see even when they were in plain sight. You thought they were a friend only to find out, when adversity appeared, they were a foe. The adversity caused you to do a self examination. It exposed hidden realities and unveiled the dynamics of relationships by revealing the hearts of people and revealing your heart too.

Are you weakling or a warrior?

In the face of adversity, we have a choice: to crumble under its weight or rise up as warriors, empowered by faith and determination.

The hardships challenge us to reassess our priorities, values, and beliefs, unveiling our inner strength and courage. The adversity will cause the unwise to become wise because we learn valuable lessons to make wiser choices, equipping us to navigate life's complexities with greater resilience.

For real, there were times I wanted to go off the deep end. I'm not going to tell you that I understood at the time what the adversity was doing for me. It was only after I came out of it that I began to understand what God was doing - three years of growth and development. It was three years of warfare and spiritual alignment. Just as Jesus dedicated three years to His ministry and fulfilled His divine assignment, my own three-year journey was filled with battles and the refining of my spirit. It was a period of intense warfare, where I had to align my life with God's purposes and align my heart with His will. The struggles and trials served for my development, shaping me into the person I am today. Despite the difficulties, I now recognize that those three years were instrumental in preparing me for the next phase of my life and ministry.

Now don't get me wrong, my church has been absolutely wonderful to me. During this particular season, we all had to come to a place of maturity. It was a time that required all of us to grow, reminiscent of the teenage years. When you start feeling yourself to assert independence and start thinking that you can do things on your own. You think that you can handle many things but life experiences have a way of humbling us to teach us otherwise. We need the guidance and the grace of God to help us with any assignment and in every aspect of our lives.

Let me be really clear if you are pastoring simply because you are upset at your former pastor you're in danger. It is important to be clear and honest about motivations. Resentment towards a former pastor can fuel a sense of bitterness and strife, which undermines the spirit of unity and love that characterizes pastoral leadership. It also distracts from the true purpose of our calling, which is to serve and shepherd God's people with humility and grace. If you are pastoring or building something for the sake of money you're in danger. A primary focus on financial gain leads astray from the true essence of ministry. While it is important to be responsible and provide for ourselves and our families, prioritizing financial gain above all else can distort priorities and compromise integrity. Ministry should be driven by a genuine desire to serve and bring about spiritual transformation, rather than being primarily motivated by financial rewards. If you build something from pain, your message, your mission, and your mind will carry the pain. You will inadvertently transmit that pain to the people who you influence. Whatever you do, whatever you build, whatever you grow, you become it with divine purpose. We operate with a divine purpose, we align ourselves with God's plan, and seek to fulfill His Will in all that we do, surrendering our own desires and agendas.

Personally, I never wanted to pastor. I never aspired to be. There were only two reasons, I believe, that someone is pastoring, either it's their calling or they're crazy! Why? The warfare that comes with this assignment will kill the average person.

The betrayal you will experience comes with the territory. The friends, family, and even money that you will lose for following His plan is tough. Nevertheless if you're called to it, you will do it with passion, love, and with care. You'll experience the greatness of God manifested in your life. You will see lives change because of the love you have for God and the people. Yes, you may lose some things but God promises those that have left all that he will restore them.

*"Then Peter began to say unto him, Lo, we have left all, and have followed thee. And Jesus answered and said, Verily I say unto you, There is no man that hath left house, or brethren, or sisters, or father, or mother, or wife, or children, or lands, for my sake, and the gospel's, but he shall receive a hundredfold now in this time, houses, and brethren, and sisters, and mothers, and children, and lands, with persecutions; and in the world to come eternal life."*
*(Mark 10:28-30 KJV)*

The warfare my wife and I experienced was heavy. There was no part of my own life that wasn't touched. My family went through such intense warfare during my pastoral journey. I lost jobs while passionately pastoring His church and building. Little did I know that the enemy would even send someone in disguise—a witch—to infiltrate our congregation, posing as a helper but with intentions to harm and pull me down. It reached my children. My children came under attack. It strained my marriage. My marriage came under attack. There was nothing that was off limits. The attacks were relentless, it seemed like there was no area left untouched.

I confess, there were moments when I walked in the church building overwhelmed by the weight of the adversity and wanted to walk right back out. The challenges seemed insurmountable. The enemy's tactics were not limited to the spiritual realm alone; my health came under attack. It was a truly trying time, my friend.

The warfare extended even to the executive team of the church. The enemy was trying to pull it apart and was relentless in his attempts to sow discord and division among us. But let me tell you, I fought with every fiber of my being. I knew that the misfits, the ones whom God had ordained in His name, were under attack. Yes, those misfits whom God said would work wonders were at war.

The enemy knows the power that lies within a united and purpose-driven team. He seeks to disrupt and dismantle that unity, knowing that when we stand together, we become a force to be reckoned with. But let me encourage you, my friend, to stand firm in the face of opposition. Recognize the tactics of the enemy and refuse to let him sow seeds of discord among your team.

Remember, the misfits are not defined by their weaknesses or shortcomings but by the transformative power of God's grace at work within them. They are the ones whom God has chosen to accomplish great things, to bring forth wonders in His name.

After one year in the new building with renovations completed, we faced a significant setback when the place flooded. It was a challenging time, we eventually got everything worked out. God favored us to move next door in the same location just a bigger space in another suite that was bigger than the one we had. As we transitioned over to the suite next door. I learned that everyone said, "Let's do it."

It's easy for people to say, "Let's do it," but true dedication and willingness to follow through are essential. Moving into the suite next door brought many benefits, as our rent and lease terms remained unchanged, but our square footage increased. The building needed some work because the previous owners that were in it had damaged the place. It wasn't up to a level of excellence that I desired to have when doing something for God. I wanted to ensure that the place we worshiped was of the highest standard, reflecting our commitment in serving God. I met with the church. I met with the team and everybody was saying, "Let's go."

When we decided to go, during this time, I faced additional challenges. I lost my job and one of the team leaders was down battling breast cancer, which meant more responsibility was back on my shoulders. Plus, unfortunately, people that said they would help, some who initially offered to help in the transition, didn't help in the transition. They were unable to follow through, so I had to grind to get it completed with little to no help. It was a period of grinding and pushing forward, I relied on my determination and faith to see the work through to completion.

I'm not saying that people that didn't help, didn't want to. They couldn't, and were unable because of job situations. I understood that and I appreciated their willingness. However, there were more people that could have helped but didn't. I was mentally drained, physically drained, and ready to quit. But I remembered! I held onto the belief that the misfits would work wonders among us. I reminded myself that quitting is not an option. God said the misfits would work wonders among me.

I don't care how bad it may get, don't you dare quit. Quitting is the language of cowards. It takes absolutely no energy to quit. It takes no focus to quit. Quitting is the easy way out and can be done with just a single thought. That's right, all it takes is just a thought to quit. On the other hand, all it takes is one thought to continue fighting and winning, too. I had made up my mind that I wasn't going to quit no matter what. Despite the challenges. I made a firm decision and committed to "No matter what!"

For the next two years, we began to experience a greater level of maturity and determination in the birth of God's people. My church began to grow in numbers. We realized that we were the sent ones and God's hand was on us.

One of the most profound and exhilarating moments etched in my memory was the midnight encounter at Bankhead Highway. It all started when I passed by the gas station on a Friday night, as usual a typical hang out night. I noticed a crowd of people parked in their cars, enjoying their music and having a party. The gas station parking lot showcased a mix of cars: Audi, Lexus, and Mercedes-Benz models, as well as older Chevys and Cutlasses. I couldn't help but notice the gathering; the gas station parking lot presented a diverse scene. Alongside the expensive cars, some people seemed to be homeless while others wore attire reminiscent of strippers. It was a lively atmosphere with loud rap music, drinking, and smoking weed, right there in the lot. A few individuals exhibited traits associated with drug dealers, with their secretive demeanor and suspicious behavior. In that instant, I felt a distinct and unmistakable prompting from the Lord, as if He whispered in my ear, "Go to them and share My message."

The urgency and conviction in His voice stirred something deep within me, igniting a passion to reach out to them and introduce them to the life-changing power of God. We gathered the people together and told them the plan of God.

The following week, fueled by the remarkable breakthrough we witnessed at the gas station, we embarked on another midnight Evangelism. This time, we ventured into one of the toughest neighborhoods in Atlanta, fully aware of the darkness that pervaded the streets. We were determined to bring the light of God's love and salvation to those who needed it most.

As we stepped into the depths of that neighborhood, we encountered a myriad of broken lives ravaged by addiction and despair. Yet, in the midst of the chaos, the power of God was undeniably at work. Drug addicts found hope in the arms of their Savior, surrendering their destructive habits for a life transformed by His grace. Even drug dealers, entangled in the web of illicit activities, were captivated by the message of redemption and turned their lives over to Christ. In a powerful display of their newfound faith I remembered one gentleman, moved by the Holy Spirit, made a decisive choice to abandon his life of drugs, threw his drugs away on the spot as a symbolic act of surrender and repentance.

The impact of our presence and everything that we committed to with the laying down the lives of our former selves through our very own transformations, including my own - the pastoring, the ministry, the misfits, our church and its purpose to do His Will - extended beyond personal transformations. Miraculously, the very atmosphere shifted, and the insidious grip of sex trafficking, which had plagued the neighborhood, was halted in its tracks. The forces of darkness retreated as the radiant light of God's love permeated the streets.

That unforgettable night, over thirty-five to forty-five individuals chose to surrender their lives to the Lord. It was a divine harvest, a tangible manifestation of the power of God in the midst of the most challenging circumstances. Our hearts rejoiced when we witnessed the miraculous work of God's grace unfolding before our very eyes.

It was in this crucible of ministry, in the heart of that tough neighborhood, that our people matured and flourished in their faith. They embraced the call to serve wholeheartedly, understanding that they were part of a divine work that could not be abandoned or compromised.

Just like Nehemiah, who faced distractions and opposition, we were resolute in our determination to press forward. We adopted his unwavering declaration, "I am doing a great work and I can't come down." We recognized that we had been entrusted with a sacred mission, a work that required our unwavering commitment and steadfast focus.

*"Now it came to pass when Sanballat, and Tobiah, and Geshem the Arabian, and the rest of our enemies, heard that I had builded the wall, and that there was no breach left therein; though at that time I had not set up the doors upon the gates; that Sanballat and Geshem sent unto me, saying, Come, let us meet together in some one of the villages in the plain of Ono. But they thought to do me mischief. And I sent messengers unto them, saying I am doing a great work, so that I cannot come down: why should the work cease, whilst I leave it, and come down to you?"*
*(Nehemiah 6:1-3 KJV)*

God was proving to us that he was with us more and more. Yes, we experience great warfare but we experience great manifestations, healing, families delivered and brought back together. There were so many miracles and prophecies that came to pass. We had to create a wall in our church to keep up with all of the prophecies.

The year 2019 drew to a close, and in those final moments, the Lord's voice resounded within my spirit. His divine directive was clear: I was to prepare His people for what was coming ahead, for something significant was on the horizon in the year 2020. He gave me specific line by line items for the people to prepare themselves. The people of God obeyed so when Covid-19 hit the people of Bethlehem City of Faith, they could testify they were already prepared. We were prepared to do ministry LIVE. God had given us the advantage over the circumstance. Covid-19 was one of the greatest things that could have ever happened to us. The pandemic strengthened us and fortified us as a church. When others thought that people wouldn't come back to church we came back stronger.

In the midst of the unfolding events in 2020, the Lord impressed upon my heart the significance of Pentecost. It was during this season that He directed me to gather His people and welcome them back to the church. Although filled with anticipation, I also harbored apprehension and fear of how others might perceive this call, especially considering the many who had chosen not to return to church during those uncertain times.

However, I understood my calling, my ministry, and my role as pastor. There was no judgment nor criticism for those who made different decisions. I just noticed that different decisions were made. Each person had to follow the leading of God according to their own faith and convictions. As the scriptures remind us, "According to thy faith be it unto you." Therefore, no judgment is casted on those who chose a different path. My focus was solely on obedience to the Lord's prompting, trusting that He would use our gathering on Pentecost to accomplish His purposes.

While the world around us was grappling with fear and uncertainty, we sought to create a space of faith, hope, and nourishment for those who felt led to return to the fellowship of believers. It was a time of stepping out in faith, putting aside the concerns of what others might think, and wholeheartedly embracing God's leading. I walk by faith and not by sight, trusting that God's wisdom surpasses all human understanding.

I heard the Lord say, "Come back!" Our decision to come back to church during that time was not motivated by financial need or a depletion of resources. It was solely driven by our obedience to the voice of the Lord. As I said earlier we gained more during Covid-19 than when the people were present.

During this period, we witnessed the faithfulness of God in a profound way. While we missed the presence of our congregation, we discovered that God's power and grace transcend physical boundaries. Yes, we had challenges like everyone else but I can testify that no one in my church died of Covid-19. As a matter of fact, no one in my church has died of anything since its inception. Glory be to God, our Father.

When God tells you to do something he backs you up. His support and provision are unfailing. With other people, it is often the case that when God instructs you to take a specific course of action, some people may hesitate or back away due to fear, doubt, or their own limitations. When God tells you to do something he will stand up when others will stand down. When God backs you up he will stop the enemy in his tracks- be the enemy and the Avenger- remaining steadfast in His commitment to see His plans fulfilled through you.

*"Out of the mouth of babes and sucklings hast thou ordained strength because of thine enemies, that thou mightest still the enemy and the avenger." (Psalms 8:2 KJV)*

I had no idea that God was about to stretch our faith and test us once again.

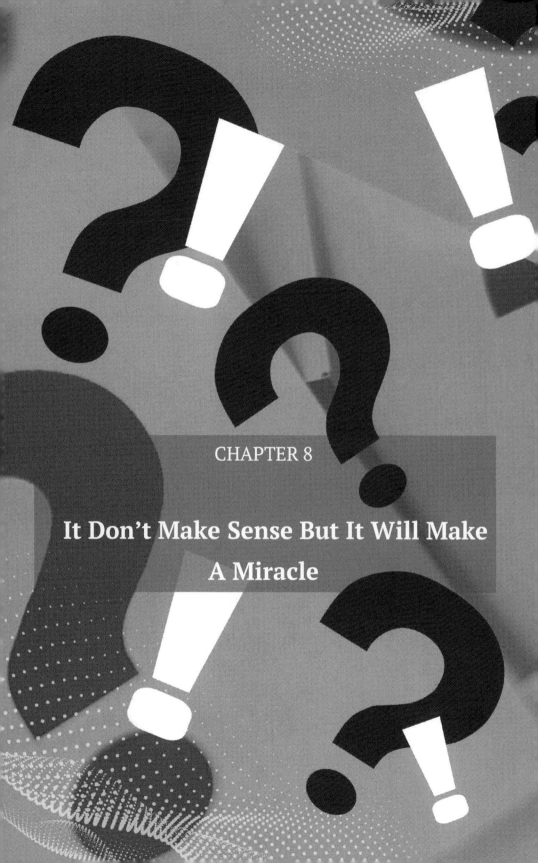

CHAPTER 8

# It Don't Make Sense But It Will Make A Miracle

*"And he entered again into the synagogue; and there was a man there, which had a withered hand. And they watched him, whether he would heal him on the sabbath day; that they might accuse him. And he saith unto the man which had the withered hand, Stand forth. And he saith unto them, Is it lawful to do good on the sabbath days, or to do evil? to save life, or to kill? But they held their peace. And when he had looked round about on them with anger, being grieved for the hardness of their hearts, he saith unto the man, Stretch forth thine hand. And he stretched it out: and his hand was restored whole as the other. And the Pharisees went forth, and straightway took counsel with the Herodians against him, how they might destroy him." (Mark 3:1-6 KJV)*

In 2021, God gave me a Word for my church. The Word was that we're going to buy a church. I need you to understand, we didn't have a whole lot of money and I had no idea where the money would come from but, I knew God told me that we were going to buy a church. Being honest we were doing good but we weren't doing great enough to buy a building. God gave me a strategy to ignite the people's faith in this vision. We were still dealing with Covid-19 and God said this. Yeah, I know it sounds crazy but God's about to give us a miracle.

The Lord gave me a strategy to raise 50k in three months, 100k in twelve months with twenty-five to thirty people during January through March. The people responded and we reached the goal in March. We rejoiced and many were crying. They were in awe of God. The people that started out with me knew where we came from and this was a big step for us. They understood the struggles and saw what we could accomplish if we did it together.

We were distinctly transparent about the finances. Every month I would share with them what we had and we kept excellent records so people could track their giving. The giving went on for about 6 months. In the month of June, I felt a strain on the people so I pulled back. I did this because I did not want them to become overwhelmed and discouraged. However a small group of us kept on giving. To be transparent I had kind of loosen or relaxed my faith in obtaining $100,000 at the end of the year. I just focused on the few that were giving and prayed for the best. We are still witnessing and feeding the homeless every single month. Things were still going quite well for the church we were building and growing. The Lord sent many confirmations that we were going to get a building like the Lord told me.

The first confirmation was by Apostle Travis C Jennings. He spoke on the night of the church anniversary and he said these words: "We are changing momentum, changing in money, changing my mission, changing in mentality, changing everything, everything about me is changing. God said get ready to change the guards, get ready to change glories, get ready to change in grace, but fourthly, get ready to change geography God said 'there is a U-Haul truck in front of this church'. Tell every witch you can. Talk about us but you will have a front row viewing cause we are getting ready to walk into the Bethlehem City of Faith".

Next confirmation was Prophet Charles Buchanan's Facebook LIVE. I just happened to be on that day, I was listening to the Word of God. Prophet Buchanan had absolutely no idea what my church was doing or who I was. He couldn't even pronounce my name. The prophet gave details as to the build and what God would do. He said these words, "I want him to sow a seed because the Lord is opening a door for a facility for a daycare for income for your ministry and you have to make some preparations and put some things in divine order because increase has hit your church".

God knew I would need those words for the journey. There was a situation that was about to appear that we did not expect at all. The lease agreement had just ended on April 18, 2021. The landlord and I had such a great relationship that we just continued to move forward as is. God had given us favor with them. Honestly, I didn't want to renew the lease because I knew God said we were going to purchase a building. I received an email from the landlord, four months later, stating that the building that we've been renting for the past few years was being sold to another company. He also informed me that he would no longer be in charge and that the new company would be. The purchase of the build was completed. My landlord continued to tell me how much he expressed to the new owners how great a tenant I was. He said they assured him that things would continue as they were. He was right, they did, so it seemed.

In the last week of October the church honored me by giving me a pastoral anniversary celebration. It was a time to receive and be blessed but little did I know that I would receive a letter stating that the new landlords were going in a different direction. I had to be out by December the 28th. We actually got the letter on the very 1st night of the anniversary. Here I was sitting there, trying to enjoy myself listening to the speakers of each night. Something each night that was said became a clue to my wife and I that God was with us.

First night it was Bishop Joanne White and she said these words, "God said he's pleased with you and like a type of Joseph you shall be, a preserve for the people. Also the Lord said wherever your foot tread he is going to give it to you". She went on to say, "It's bigger and better. Don't you stress yourself because God has raised you up for increase. Lastly don't forget you are a Prophet and when you prophesy it is going to move".

She had no idea I was sweating bullets because once again an unexpected move had to happen. Also, I was reminded that I prophesied at the beginning of the year we were getting a building.

The second night Prophet Raymond Randle said this, "I see you acquiring land and I see you really building but it's not. It doesn't look like a conventional church, it's a couple of buildings, and it was not a traditional building. The land that you're gonna purchase that's gonna come into your hand, It gonna be a steal.

God said I am sending you some sustainers to help you sustain until you're ready."

Those words from God were mind blowing; everything that was said we will speak on later. So now Sunday has come and we have two worship services left. The end of service arrived for the first service and my wife and I are dreading telling the people what's ahead. Those first two nights of the celebration were tough for me. I was trying to enjoy it but I was concerned about the dilemma we had. We had approximately fifty to sixty days to exit the property. So I had the media crew cut off streaming services so that I could talk to the congregation about the situation.

My heart was heavy. As I stood behind the pulpit with anticipation of how the congregation would respond to the news I was about to share. I called my wife to stand with me, and the people braced themselves, knowing that I had a significant announcement to make. With the letter in my hand, I began reading it aloud, revealing that we needed to vacate the premises by December 28th. The people began to rejoice at such a high level that it was mind-blowing. They were rejoicing at the fact that someone was telling us to leave and they believed that God was going to move for their pastor. I can't begin to tell you how encouraging that was to know that the people of God had my back and were going to stick with me through this situation. Sometimes we have plans but God has other plans. I had foreseen us moving but at a slower pace than what the dilemma presented. God is so amazing! I left the church ready to come back for the night service because I knew God was going to say something else to us. This night was going to be sensational.

My spiritual father, Bishop Paul L. Fortson was the last speaker. During his time the bishop began to give his testimony about purchasing a building. I had not discussed anything with him about my dilemma. My people, that I pastor, just found out a few hours ago we had to leave the building because the landlord was going in a different direction. They were sitting here in this service. They were hearing the similarities of my bishop's testimony and what we were dealing with presently. They began to rejoice. The bishop spoke about how he only had forty-five days to find a place and God moved for him. God allowed Bishop Fortson to purchase a half a million dollar property with just a handful of people. When my people heard his testimony they rejoiced even more.

That night this is what the bishop said, "I speak favor over you, don't worry about the money for favor is on you. Son, you're gonna need another place, don't worry about it, go look." Then, pointing at the congregation he said, "These eyes should be looking too; they should be praying and be faithful". The bishop continued, "When the Lord told me we were gonna leave our pretty little blue church I was shocked it was pretty just like your church, pastor".

I remember the Lord said, "In one year you will be gone".

I told the church we were leaving in one year but two weeks before the year we had nowhere to go. The congregation rose to their feet in praise, pointing, and shouting to the bishop letting him know he was reading our mail. Like him, we had nowhere to go. The bishop continued his testimony.

Someone spoke out loud and said to him, "No, we're gonna stay here".

The bishop replied "No we will not! If I gotta preach on the street, I will do it, but we are not going to stay here." The bishop turned to me and said, "When God says it's up, it's up".

The congregation responded back to him saying, "I didn't know where I was going but I wasn't gonna stay there. I stayed long enough. I loved that place but it was time to go".

The bishop had no idea what was happening until we told him a little later and the power of God fell in that place in such a tremendous way. The bishop laid his hands on my hands and prayed. Before I knew it, I was laying face down because the overwhelming presence of God was on me. I laid there crying because the presence of God was strong. I tried getting up and I ended up going back down to my knees on the floor again. The Lord began to minister to me saying, "I am with you and you will not fail". Over and over He kept saying this as I'm weeping laying on the floor in the presence of God. The people of God really began to give toward our building project and truth be told, we did it, we had enough to buy a building.

In those awe-inspiring moments, we were reminded that with God, all things are possible. We had witnessed His power, experienced His presence, and received His reassurance that He was with us, guiding us into the fulfillment of His plans. It was a time of overwhelming gratitude and humility as we marveled at the goodness of our God.

The journey had been challenging, marked by warfare and uncertainty, but through it all, God's faithfulness remained steadfast. We stood in awe of His provision and knew that His promises never fail. We pressed forward, ready to embrace the next chapter of our church's journey.

I contacted my commercial real estate agent who had helped me get the building that we were currently in. I told her my plans and to my surprise she was not in support of us buying. She told me that we were too young of a church for any bank to give us a loan.

"I know you don't know me or my ministry but we don't look at the problem," I said to her, "we focus on the solution and we walk by faith. I'm a man of faith, what is impossible to man will be possible to God".

"Yeah," She replied back, "I know but you got to also look at what the banks say and what reality is".

She looked at a few buildings for us but I could tell that her heart wasn't for us. She expressed a lot of doubt and skepticism about our ability to purchase. She gave me a long speech emphasizing how challenging it would be for us to secure a building and citing examples of other churches that had rented for years to save money.

I respectfully disagreed with her perspective, encouraging her to reconsider her own pastor's approach. I could tell that my faith bothered her. I expressed that it shouldn't take fifteen years to raise funds for a church when faith in God's provision is at work. My belief in God's ability to accomplish great things seemed to unsettle her, as if my faith challenged her own understanding and expertise. She looked at me with a mix of surprise and skepticism as if to say how dare I tell her that I was going to get a building. She appeared offended that I would dare to believe in something bigger than what she deemed possible based on her experience.

Despite her reservations and the doubts she expressed, I remained steadfast. I understood that walking in faith often means going against conventional wisdom and even the opinions of others. I was determined to trust in God's leadership and provision, confident that He would open the right doors and make a way for us to obtain a building for our church. Eventually, I made the decision to part ways with her.

I stepped out on faith and asked my real estate agent who sold me my house to help me. She immediately said, "Pastor I'm walking with you and I'm believing in God with you". Her name was Natasha. She was God's woman for the job. Together, we began searching for potential properties. We came across one property that seemed promising and we felt a strong conviction from God about it. However, we learned that someone else had already put a contract on it. Undeterred, we decided to put in a contract as well, trusting that God would make a way for us.

Despite our efforts, we didn't end up securing that particular property.

I stumbled upon another property that I had recently looked over and I really didn't pay much attention to the details because by the looks of it, it wasn't much. As I began to really look at it I noticed that it was huge. I also noticed that there were two buildings on the property. I knew that the building didn't pass the eye test, which is important, but it had potential. My wife and I scheduled a showing and I could see what God was doing. Every prophecy that was released I was walking in at that moment. I knew that was the place.

I called for a meeting, a fellowship dinner with my executive team, and handed each one a flier of the place and told them my vision for the place. A few of the partners were skeptical but supportive. The majority was with it. They all said to me, "Pastor you haven't led us wrong yet and we trust your wisdom".

We prepared the offer on the building. It was two buildings on twelve acres of land. It was over half a million. My wife said to me, "Don't offer that, offer this".

Seriously, my wife 's faith leaves me in awe and, at times, makes me feel a bit uneasy. She isn't afraid to believe in God for the craziest things. You see, she possesses a fearless belief in God that stretches beyond the boundaries of what some might consider reasonable or practical. It's in her faith that the most incredible things have unfolded, and what is truly amazing is that

God has responded to her with astounding displays of His power and provision.

I asked her, "Are you sure?"

Without hesitation, she looked me in the eyes and confidently replied, "Yes!"

We went for it and put in the offer. Crazy faith.

We waited for the owners to respond to our offer. There was no response for weeks. The clock was ticking on us and we didn't have a whole lot of time to waste. Nevertheless, we held on to our faith.

Finally a response came. The response was that we have others that want the building as well. It was a developer who was willing to pay cash for the building. The news of another interested party, caused my heart to sink into my belly with a mix of concern and uncertainty. It seemed as though the odds were stacked against us, for we didn't possess the financial resources to compete on that level. Yet, in the depths of my being, I knew that this building was destined to be ours. At that moment, however, faith beat the facts.

How in the world were we going to beat a 'cash on hand' buyer?

I came home after work hearing that news and I prayed. The Lord said to me, "I have given you two buildings and twelve acres".

I got up and I told my wife what the Lord said. We stood on that Word. We kept our faith. All we had was a Word from the

Lord we didn't have cash to buy out right. We didn't flinch or balk on the offer. The offer had been on the table for two weeks now. We heard absolutely nothing. We kept standing on what God said, "I have given you two buildings and twelve acres". We had to be fearless in the face of uncertainty, we chose to walk by faith and not by sight.

Being fearless is experiencing fears, but not being afraid to face it, or retreat. The voice in your head says, "You can't win, it's too big, or it's too bad", but faith over powers what's in your head so you can have it in your hands. Here is a thought: your faith will one day meet up with your fear and the reality is one will win. Faith has a remarkable way of defying logic and transcending earthly limitations. It invites us to fix our gaze not on the visible obstacles but on the invisible hand of God that moves in mysterious ways. It beckons us to believe in the supernatural, the realm where miracles are born and impossibilities become opportunities for divine intervention. It's totally up to you. Anything is possible if you believe.

My agent Natasha texted me one morning and said, "Pastor, I need to talk to you".

"Sure," I replied, "Give me a call".

When she calls me and tells me, "Pastor, I had a dream and in the dream you were in the building and you were laying down a gray carpet. I saw the people working to lay down new carpet and your Deacon Brad was helping. I normally don't dream stuff like this but I know it's God telling us that everything is going to work out".

I know this sounds crazy but her dream is important you will see later.

I went to church a few days later and someone wanted to meet with me. This person who wanted to remain anonymous came to me and said, "the Lord told me to sow this seed".

I opened the envelope and it was 50k. I was overwhelmed with emotion. I was speechless because of the level of faith they demonstrated and the trust they had in God. To this day, I think about that often. God used someone I didn't expect to sow an over the top seed. That night after I finished teaching bible study I heard the Lord tell me to go down to the property and anoint the mailbox with anointed oil. I know it sounds crazy but it's about to make a miracle. I believed He told me to go by myself and don't tell anyone but my wife. He knew if I told them that they would want to go with me but God wanted this to be between him and I.

With a sense of awe and anticipation, I drove down to the property. As I arrived, I saw that there were people having a function in the building, attending an event hosted by a small church renting the space. So I turned around, understanding the need for divine timing, I retreated to a nearby gas station. Until I heard the Holy Spirit tell me to go, I sat there and waited for about ten minutes. Then the Holy Spirit said, "They're all gone now".

Let me tell you the Holy Spirit is the most neglected function in the body of Christ but the Holy Spirit is my best friend. As I embarked on the journey to the property, I was acutely aware of the Holy Spirit's leading in every step. It is through the Holy Spirit that God communicates His divine will and imparts wisdom and discernment to His children. The Holy Spirit is not merely an abstract concept but a vibrant, living presence, intimately involved in every aspect of our lives. I pulled up to the property and just like the Holy Spirit said the cars were gone.

Nervous, filled with anticipation, I hopped out of my car, and walked up to the mailbox. In my trembling hand, I held a small bottle of anointing oil, a symbol of God's consecration and blessing, put a little on my finger, and made a pentecostal cross shape on the mailbox. As I began to walk away the Holy Spirit said to me, "No, pour the entire bottle on the mailbox". So I poured the entire contents of that bottle of anointing oil on the mailbox, an act that seemed unconventional and even audacious. Yet, in that moment, I recognized the unmistakable prompting of God's Spirit, guiding me to step out in radical obedience. I hopped in my car and sped off. I was thinking to myself that was crazy but I knew God told me to do it.

After anointing their mailbox, three days later, the owners of the building accepted my offer. Wow! I told the people and we rejoiced, God had done it again. Not only did we have the money we needed to go forward and the financial paperwork in place to show we were serious about purchasing, but we were also equipped with meticulous and organized financial paperwork that showcased our commitment and seriousness in acquiring the property. It was a testament to the importance of strategic planning and foresight. A few years back God led me to secure a firm with excellent record keeping when we did not have much, resources were limited. It was a sacrifice, as it involved allocating funds towards professional assistance when there were other pressing needs within our church. However, little did we know at the time that this investment would prove instrumental in our current journey.

One of the things that a leader must do is be integral and transparent about the finances at all times. I firmly believe in the importance of integrity and transparency when it comes to handling the finances of God's house. It is crucial to maintain open and honest communication with the congregation. Surround yourself with trusted leaders that will keep you accountable. We must handle God's business with excellence. It's more than just Sunday morning and praise breaks. It encompasses a broader scope that extends to the careful execution of excellence in every aspect of God's house. From budgeting and financial planning to resource allocation and responsible spending, we strive to maintain the highest standards of financial management. I will execute excellence with God's house.

Recognizing the significance, I took the responsibility of presenting our financial records to the banker, as it was a necessary requirement. As I sat in his office, he carefully reviewed the documents, his gaze would occasionally shift from the paperwork to meet my eyes. This exchange repeated several times, and I couldn't help but feel a sense of apprehension building within me. He glanced to look at me. Again, he does the same.

Looks at my paperwork then he looks at me and says, "You've been pastoring just for 6 years". In my head I'm thinking uh-oh this is what my first faithless real estate agent warned me about that we weren't old enough to get a building.

With a mix of anticipation and anxiety, I was frozen but responded to his inquiry, "Yes, Sir!", confirming that I had indeed been pastoring for only six years. Internally, I braced myself for what might come next, fearing that our perceived lack of experience might jeopardize our chances of securing a building. The weight of the moment hung heavy in the air as I awaited his response.

"That is amazing." He responded back, "That you have kept these types of records and financial reports".

"Yes sir!"

"Thank you, Mr. Eichelberger, that's all I need. We will work with the underwriting and then we will call you".

To my surprise, the banker's words were not ones of skepticism or doubt. Instead, he expressed genuine admiration, emphasizing the exceptional quality of our financial records and reports. I felt a wave of relief wash over me as I realized that our commitment to maintaining detailed accuracy with the financials had not gone unnoticed. Humbly, I acknowledged his compliment and thanked him for his kind words, relieved that our meticulous record-keeping had left a positive impression.

Two to three days later he called, "We have a deal for you and here's your financial responsibilities". The banker's call came bearing the news we had been eagerly anticipating. We had no problems handling any financial responsibilities. We had started sowing in January when God said so and never stopped even when things got tough. The journey had not been without its trials and tribulations. There were moments when the path seemed uncertain, and doubts threatened to overshadow our faith. Yet, in those moments of doubt, we held firm to the promises of God and pressed on

I took some of my executive team men with me to view the property that we had a new contract with now. We had sown, we had believed, and now we were reaping the harvest of His promises. Our hearts were filled with gratitude as we embraced the next chapter of our journey.

Everyone was excited and started to see the vision that God had given us. We went through all of the necessary steps of inspecting the build, checking everything. My agent was phenomenal. During the inspection process, we carefully assessed the property and identified a few areas that required attention and repair. It was a critical phase in the purchasing process, as these findings could potentially impact the final price of the building. It was at this point that my wife's unwavering faith, which often made me cringe with amazement, came into play once again.

As my wife and I discussed our options, I said to her, "I think if we present these items to the owner they will knock down the price. For this amount."

However, my wife, fueled by her faith, had a different perspective. She confidently asserted, "No, ask for this much off instead."

I am telling you, I asked for 10K. She asked for 40K. I was taken aback, as her suggested amount exceeded my expectations by a significant margin. I hesitantly suggested we present to them a reduction offering of $10,000.

My heart filled with excitement when my sweet wife said to me, "No babe, send it back", while she boldly proposed a reduction of $40,000. I shook my head in disbelief, but deep down, I knew her faith had often moved mountains in our journey thus far.

I said, "That's good".

She said, "I know but they can do more for you".

I stared at her for about ten seconds and smiled, "Ok!" Only she can do that and captivate me as I gazed into her eyes amazed by her belief in God's ability to do the impossible. I said, "We'll send it back."

Together, we made the decision to send back our offer, not settling for the modest reduction I had originally suggested. It was a moment of surrendering to God's plan, relinquishing our own preconceived notions, and embracing faith. In that simple act of obedience, we positioned ourselves to witness the miraculous hand of God at work. Little did we know that our act of faith would pave the way for a remarkable turn of events. Our decision to aim higher and ask for more became the catalyst for God's favor to pour out upon us. The days that followed were marked by eager anticipation, as we awaited the response to our revised offer. Finally, the long-awaited response arrived, carrying with it the confirmation of God's faithfulness. The owners had not only accepted our revised offer. They had gone above and beyond our wildest expectations, it came back with an additional reduction, 20K more. God did it again.

Keep people around you that will believe God has more for you. It is of utmost importance to surround ourselves with individuals who wholeheartedly believe in God's abundant blessings and His desire to do more for us. In particular, when we are blessed with a life partner, we have found a precious gift and a source of invaluable support. If you found a wife, you found a good thing, and you found your help. Our wives are not only our companions but also our helpers, entrusted by God to walk alongside us in every aspect of our lives. Especially as Pastors, it is easy to fall into the trap of shouldering the burdens alone and thinking that we have to handle everything on our own. However, this couldn't be further from the truth. God has gifted us with a wife who is not only our partner in life but also our partner in ministry. Never let your wife feel isolated from a process that she was called to help in. This is why God gave us a helpmeet. I appreciate my wife and the beautiful partnership that God intended. With the unique gifts she possesses along with her insights, wisdom, and faith, my wife has greatly enriched and strengthened our journey. To isolate our wives from the processes and decisions that impact our ministry would be a disservice. When we embrace their involvement, we tap into a wellspring of love, support, and spiritual guidance that can propel us to new heights. She helps make me better and is also known to the church as Lady T.

On December 28th, which was the deadline, we had to get out of the building. Long story short, we found favor with the landlord. He, recognizing our circumstances, allowed us to stay until we had our New Year's Eve celebration. Afterwards, friends of ours allowed us an opportunity to transition into their church, River of Living Water Word Church, until God blessed us to close.

Pastor Derrick and Falisha Smith are amazing people of God. They opened their doors and hearts to us, welcoming our congregation with open arms. It was a time of unity even though closing on the building proved to be another challenge, particularly in the midst of the ongoing COVID-19 pandemic. They told us we would close on one date, we didn't. We kept going back and forth. The process was filled with uncertainties and unexpected delays. My banker assured me that it had nothing to do with the church. There were challenges between the banks and the owner. I don't know why to this day. We prayed and believed in God, that's all we did. Eventually, they gave us another date,

January 27th. Yet, even then the enemy was trying to stop that to hinder our progress because the closing lawyer caught Covid-19.

Nevertheless we found favor in the eyes of God and we closed via Zoom on January the 27th 2021. We closed on two buildings and twelve acres. Immediately we got in the car, my wife and I, and right behind us, the real estate agent. We went to the new property we just purchased, looked at all other things that we have to do, took a few photos and went on our way out. There was something interesting that I discovered on the way out that I didn't see on my way into the property. When I looked to my left, as we're leaving, I noticed that the mailbox had been totally destroyed. It was as if someone took a baseball bat and beat it until it broke. It seemed as though an invisible force relentlessly pummeled it until it shattered. Now remember God had told me to anoint the mailbox. Yes, I know it's crazy to some but that obedience to God shifted something in that region. I believe that a demonic presence was holding up our progress. God delivered and the enemy came to destroy an altar that was built in honor of God. Nevertheless we won. God does things that don't make sense but it will make a miracle.

Looking back on this journey, we are reminded of the faithfulness of our God. He orchestrated every detail, aligned the right people, and opened doors that no one could shut. It was a testament to His power, His grace, and His unwavering love for His people.

In the end, we stand in awe of God's faithfulness and goodness. He proved once again that He is a God of miracles, and He will never leave us nor forsake us. As we continue to move forward in our new building, we do so with hearts filled with gratitude, knowing that every step was guided by His hand.

*"But God hath chosen the foolish things of the world to confound the wise; and God hath chosen the weak things of the world to confound the things which are mighty." (1 Corinthians 1:27 KJV)*

God kept releasing a flow of extraordinary miracles through the hands of Paul. Because of this, people took Paul's handkerchiefs and articles of clothing, even pieces of cloth that had touched his skin, laying them on the bodies of the sick, and diseases and demons left them and they were healed. (*see Acts 19:11-12 KJV*)

It looked crazy, it looked like we were in trouble but God gave us a miracle.

CHAPTER 9

**We started But God Isn't Finished!**
**Crazy Right?**

*"And it came to pass, when our enemies heard that it was known unto us, and God had brought their counsel to nought, that we returned all of us to the wall, every one unto his work."*
*(Nehemiah 4:15 KJV)*

It didn't dawn on me until months later, I had a profound realization about the significance of my initial trial message being from the book of Nehemiah. "Build the wall" echoed in my mind, and I realized the parallel between Nehemiah's task and my own journey. I was not walking out what I preached, concerning Nehemiah, I was now building and strategizing. This book holds a special place in my heart; it is one of my favorites. It serves as a constant reminder of the mission I've undertaken and the faith I've placed in God's plan. It continues to provide me with the strategies and wisdom necessary in struggles to overcome obstacles and complete the work I believe God has given me to do.

On January 30th, I surprised my church with the incredible news - we had closed on our new building and we were ready to go. I jokingly called a meeting after church and told them I had an announcement to make. No one knew that we had closed except for Bishop Fortson, my wife and my real estate agent, Natasha. I pretended like I was going to give them a gift for all the hard work they had been doing with helping us transition into this temporary location. In front of the people, I handed each of my two deacons a blue envelope.

"Open the envelope," I said, "What's in this envelope belongs to you".

Looking at me bewildered and confused, the deacons of my church reached in the envelope and pulled out a set of keys.

"Shout and rejoice", I said to them, "because we just got the keys to our new church and those are your personal keys to the building."

The moment the church heard this news, an eruption of praise and excitement filled the air. Tears of joy flowed freely as the realization of what God had done for us came to fruition. People were hugging each other and crying, "God had given us a miracle". It was a celebration of hearts overflowing with gratitude for God's mighty work.

Now the physical work begins. God had given me clear instructions of who to put in charge of the work while I would be working. The Lord had given me the name of one deacon that would oversee the renovations being done at our new location. Two weeks after the closing, we eagerly embarked on the work ahead. We gathered the people together to start on a Saturday morning. Together, we walked the property, surveying the building, and its surroundings. Sensing the significance of the moment, I called everyone to seek God's guidance and blessings through prayer. We decided two weeks after the closing to start the work. The people rallied together excited about starting. We gathered the people together to start the work on a Saturday morning. The people were coming in, walking around the property, and examining    the building. When they finished, I called everyone to the sanctuary to pray. We formed a circle and we began to pray. When we finished praying, the mother of one of the daughters of my church came and hugged me. As she hugged me, she began to praise and speak in tongues; she did the same to my wife. I left out the doors momentarily to retrieve some tools. Then people started to disperse. I became unaware of the tragic turn that awaited me.

I was startled when someone ran behind me as I was going to my car. It was a woman unknown to me. She had been chasing after me to deliver devastating news and then said to me, "Phylis, the mother of one of the members in the church, had passed out".

I rushed back, my heart heavy with worry, to discover that she had died. In the midst of chaos, one of the deacons of the church and I administered CPR while urgently calling for paramedics. Despite our efforts, she departed this world, leaving behind an atmosphere of sorrow and grief.

Now I want you to really understand how the death of a woman had a profound impact on the work of the church. The enemy, in his relentless pursuit, had strategically planned to discourage, hinder, and stop what God had divinely ordained to happen. The congregation, His people, who had been rejoicing with hopeful anticipation, went from that rejoicing to suddenly being immersed in a wave of crying and sadness. There was a heaviness in the place, dampening spirits and challenging the resiliency of the community.

One of the deacons came to me and said, "Let's send the people home. It seemed like the right thing to do but never do anything without consulting God".

As I distanced myself from the gathering crowd at the door, the Lord spoke to me, "Do not stop." In that moment, I realized that despite the tragic circumstances and the controversial nature of the decision, God was urging me to press forward. I turned back to the deacon and the crowd and I boldly declared, "We shall not stop, we will continue with the work. Let's go!"

It was a very controversial decision because someone had died. This decision carried great weight, for it challenged the conventional understanding of pausing in the face of death. Yet, with unwavering faith and trust, we continued because God told me to continue and I believed that the woman of God was going to live. Long story short, we went to the hospital to find that medical professionals had detected a pulse in the woman, a sign that life still flickered within her. This small but significant development validated our decision to continue with the work. The doctors were saying it was only temporary and she wouldn't make it. I prophesied to my congregation and the family and I told them, "Do not hang your heads because your mother will walk out that hospital and be well. She will live and not die to declare the works of the Lord". Through following God's prompting, and against all odds, the woman's life was preserved. She's alive and well and thriving.

When bad things happen in the midst of building and evolving you must always move in faith. Move in faith even when the facts look more convincing than the faith. Don't stay still. Don't look at the problem, God always has the solution.  Don't let nothing paralyze purpose. You may not have time to go to a prayer closet and seek God for four hours to answer a situation that just happened in five minutes. I had to make a decision as a leader, as a visionary, right on the spot. I am sure many judged my decision as negative. God backed my decision with a miracle. Faith activates God to move on your behalf.

God favored us. It seemed every single day that we were working on renovating the church. We stepped into a Nehemiah experience where the place was in bad shape. However we continued working, praying, and believing in God. One of the things that really got my attention is when we were selling the pews out of the chapel. A white gentleman came to pick up the pews. Now at the time, I was at home getting myself ready to come to the church and work. One of the men already at the church sent me a picture of this white man at our church and he wasn't picking up the pews, instead picked up a paint brush and began to work with the members of my church. I was shocked. Again God sent someone out of nowhere but this time to help us do this work.

When I eventually arrived at the building, I had the opportunity to meet this man of God who happened to be a pastor. As I stood at the door, He said these words to me: "I immediately felt the presence of God. I also felt that it was my duty to help with the work that God was doing through your church". As he continued talking he pointed at the building with the paintbrush in hand and said to me, "Man of God, you are picking up another man's work that has expired and you're launching a new vision. I want you to be encouraged because I can tell you just by the presence I felt, God is with you".

Gathering my people together, I shared the words of encouragement that he just shared with me and everyone was encouraged. The atmosphere was charged and renewed as everyone recognized God orchestrating our journey. God even used Pastor John once again. He showed up to the work site and said to me, "I'm here to help. Whatever you need. We're going to get it done and just continue to move forward".

God's blessings continued to pour out abundantly as He sent one person after another to support us in our journey. Among the most significant and impactful moments was when my godson's father, who owns an electrical company, graciously conducted a walk-through of the building. As he assessed the code violations, outdated lights, and equipment, it seemed as though he would provide an estimate for the necessary work. However, to my astonishment, he went above and beyond by sending his employees from It's Electric, led by Mr. Borom, the owner himself of our building.

Their dedicated team tirelessly worked from sunup to sundown, investing their skills and time to complete an estimated

20k to 30k worth of electrical work free of charge. This thoughtful gesture left an indelible mark on my heart, and I will forever be grateful for their selfless act of kindness. The generosity and support extended by Mr. Borom and his company not only alleviated the financial burden but also exemplified the power of community and God's provision in our endeavor. We dedicated ourselves to a month-long endeavor to renovate and enhance our church building. The amount of trash and debris we had to remove was substantial, and it took four thirty-foot dumpsters to contain it all. However, our efforts went beyond physical labor. We understood the importance of prayer and came together to seek guidance and strength from a higher power. With a unified mindset and unwavering determination, we tackled the task at hand, knowing that through our collective efforts and reliance on prayer, we would achieve our goal. This collaborative approach, coupled with our faith, allowed us to successfully complete phase one of the renovation within the allotted time frame.

*"So we built the wall; and all the wall was joined together unto the half thereof: for the people had a mind to work."*
*(Nehemiah 4:6 KJV)*

On that momentous day, March 20th, our hearts overflowed with gratitude as we held our very first service in our new location. To God alone belongs all the glory for the incredible journey we have embarked upon. We witnessed firsthand the power of God as He performed our first miracle, raising a woman from the clutches of death. Miracles, signs, and wonders are a regular occurrence at Bethlehem City of Faith Church.

In the midst of our endeavors, I acknowledge that to some, it may seem as if we are taking unconventional and even crazy steps. Yet, I stand firm in the knowledge that it's all God's doing. Yes, I know I look crazy but it's all God. I understand that it may appear wild and illogical, but mark my words, I know it may look crazy but it's going to make a miracle.

In this year alone, as we settled into our new building, God surprised me once again with a seemingly outrageous command: to pay off the entire building within such a short time. From January to March, we embarked on a journey of raising the necessary funds, fully trusting that God's presence and provision would be with us every step of the way. It may appear crazy to the world, but I firmly believe that it will be the catalyst for a miraculous manifestation of God's faithfulness.

Whenever you find yourself in our area, I encourage you to come and visit Bethlehem City of Faith Church. Experience firsthand the wonders that unfold within our walls. Witness the power of God in action and be inspired by the atmosphere of faith and expectancy. Finally, keep your eyes open. There may be a next book, as we continue to chronicle the next chapters of our incredible journey. Anticipate further revelations of God's goodness and the miraculous works He has in store for us. Remember, even if it may seem crazy, I know it's all God. I know that He is with us, and I know that despite how it may appear, it's going to bring forth a miracle that will leave us in awe.

In Conclusion my prayer is that this book has inspired and catapulted you to new levels in faith. I want you to follow the lead of God no matter how big the assignment is, no matter who says it won't work. Trust me I have been there. You may look crazy doing it but you would be crazy not to follow the plan of God.

Remain in Crazy Faith.

**Jameson Eichelberger**